PLAYING SIT-&-GO POKER

POKER

AS A

BUSINESS

A SERIOUS PLAYER'S MANUAL FOR MAKING BIG MONEY LIVE AND ONLINE

T0108833

ABOUT ROB TUCKER

Rob Tucker moved from New York City to Toronto to earn his M.B.A. from the Schulich School Of Business. It was while earning his degree that he discovered what a great city Toronto is for poker players. Rob quickly took to the no-limit hold'em games in the five casinos in and around the city, in the host of Toronto's live private games, and online. He soon realized that his decision to move to Toronto was a wise one. Rob has been a regular winner in cash games and both online and live sit-and goes for years, and has at last written this book on his unique approach to winning money at sit-and-go poker. He is also the author of the highly regarded *Playing No-Limit Hold'em as a Business*.

PLAYING SIT-&-GO POKER AS A BUSINESS

ROB TUCKER

A SERIOUS PLAYER'S MANUAL FOR
MAKING BIG MONEY LIVE AND ONLINE

CARDOZA PUBLISHING

GAMBLER'S BOOK CLUB

Get all your gambling books at Gambler's Book Club in Las Vegas, and enjoy the world's largest selection of gambling books, software, and information—more than 3,000 titles in stock!
www.gamblersbookclub.com

FREE POKER & GAMING MAGAZINES!
www.cardozabooks.com

Sign up now to read all about the exciting world of poker, gambling, and online gaming. Our free online magazines are packed with tips, expert strategies, tournament schedules and results, gossip, news, contests, polls, prepublication book discounts, free-money bonuses for online sites, words of wisdom from the world's top experts and authorities, and much more! And what's best—it's FREE! Visit us now!

Cardoza Publishing is the foremost gaming and gambling publisher in the world with a library of more than 200 up-to-date and easy-to-read books and strategies. These authoritative works are written by the top experts in their fields and with more than 10,000,000 books in print, represent the best-selling and most popular gaming books anywhere.

FIRST EDITION
Copyright © 2011 by Rob Tucker

Library of Congress Catalog Number: 2010933127
ISBN 10:   1-58042-265-9
ISBN 13: 978-1-58042-265-9

Visit our website or write for a full list of Cardoza Publishing books and advanced strategies.

CARDOZA PUBLISHING
P.O. Box 98115, Las Vegas, NV 89193
Toll-Free Phone (800)577-WINS
email: cardozabooks@aol.com
www.cardozabooks.com

T TABLE OF CONTENTS

1 INTRODUCTION

The moneymaking system in this book is an untapped secret in the poker world. You can use this dynamic system to significantly increase your profits playing poker.

You will learn not only how to be successful playing no-limit hold'em sit-and-go tournaments, but how to make money from them in a way that you might not realize exists. Poker players who are familiar with this profit generating approach are mostly experienced professionals or others who have tried to win a seat into the World Series of Poker or other big money events like the World Poker Tour.

However, you don't have to be a professional player to make a business out of playing sit-and-goes. I'll show you how to win using the secret strategies the pros have been guarding for far too long.

I have made a lot of money using the exact strategies you'll learn in this book. That's why I can confidently say that my method is the most reliable, fun and profitable strategy you can use to repeatedly turn profits at single-table satellites. I have done this for years. After reading this book, you can too.

2 THE ROADMAP TO BIG PROFITS

This book teaches you how to play two types of sit-and-go events:

1. **Live Single-Table Sit-And-Go Satellites to Win Entry Into Big-Money No-Limit Hold'em Tournaments.** The strategies I give you for winning live one-table satellites will empower you to consistently finish in the top two of a single-table sit-and-go for which the top prize is a Main Event seat valued at $10,000. Particular emphasis is put on the deal making that occurs between the final two players. Therein lies the secret in this book— it is from this deal making that you will earn big money faster and easier than you ever have before playing no-limit hold'em.

2. **Online Single-Table Sit-and-Go Tournaments to Win Cash Prizes.** If you have played online poker, you've probably played online sit-and-go tournaments for cash profit. However, in case you are new to the game, I explain how online sit-and-go tournaments work, how to win money from them, and how to build on your experience playing them to make even more money playing sit-and-go satellites. First, I explain the similarities and

differences between traditional online sit-and-goes and live satellite sit-and-goes, followed by lessons on how to consistently finish in the money playing traditional online sit-and-goes.

A UNIQUE AND POWERFUL SATELLITE GAME PLAN

After discussing traditional online sit-and-goes, I get into the real meat of the book, my proven strategies for winning live, two-level, sit-and-go satellites. I explain the format for the profitable satellites I recommend you play, and dedicate most of the book to successful strategies for playing them.

By using this powerful new game plan, you will bring a far more optimistic and confident attitude to the table than your opponents. While the lessons in this book are all business, you will feel confident navigating satellites using a roadmap designed to earn you big payoffs. And since the number of big buy-in tournaments continues to grow, you will find no shortage of opportunities to profit from these satellites.

MAKING DEALS THAT WILL LINE YOUR POCKETS WITH PROFIT

Making deals in sit-and-go satellites is a great way to guarantee that you walk away with some money—even if you don't win the satellite—and ensure that you continue to profit from playing poker. Maybe you've played in live satellites before, perhaps even winning your way into a big-money tournament such as a World Poker Tour event or the World Series of Poker Main Event. If so, you may have engaged in making a deal, also called a "chop." Other professional players and I take this deal making quite seriously. In fact, the process can even be a lot of fun. I outline a mock negotiation scenario that shows you exactly what you need to think about and say to your opponent in order to earn the profit you so richly deserve.

ODDS AND PROBABILITIES

At the end of the book, I give you some important pointers on pot odds and how to calculate probabilities. I've designed this section to help you more perfectly and easily execute the basic strategy of winning sit-and-goes.

Now, let's get down to the nuts and bolts of the business of winning satellites. I'll show you how to win bigger profits than you ever imagined—and you can take that to the bank!

3

TRADITIONAL SIT-&-GO TOURNAMENTS AND SIT-&-GO SATELLITES—WHAT'S THE DIFFERENCE?

There are differences between traditional online sit-and-go tournaments and one-table, two-step sit-and-go satellites.

TRADITIONAL ONLINE SIT-AND-GO TOURNAMENTS

A standard online sit-and-go tournament is a nine-player event that begins as soon as nine players sign up. The objective in nine-person online sit-and-goes is to make a profit by finishing in the money, which is usually the top three. If you finish in fourth place or worse, you do not get paid so you lose your buy-in.

Here is an example of how the money is paid out in an online sit-and-go tournament. Let's say the buy-in is $50 plus $5. This means that you are investing a total of $55, of which $50 goes into the prize pool and $5 goes to the poker site. With nine players there is $450 in the prize pool, of which the winner usually receives 50 percent ($225), the runner up receives 30 percent ($135), and third place receives 20 percent

> You make your profits in standard sit-and-go tournaments by finishing in the top three.

CARDOZA PUBLISHING ♠ ROB TUCKER

($90). As you can see, playing online sit-and-goes is all about going deep so you can finish in the money and earn a profit.

TWO-STEP SIT-AND-GO SATELLITES

A sit-and-go satellite is a sit-and-go poker game that you play to win a seat into a big tournament that has a more expensive buy-in. It begins as soon as nine or ten players have signed up for it, depending on whether you are playing online (nine players) or live (ten players).

Some satellites are two-step events in which you gain entry into the second step by winning the first step. Then if you win the second step, you win a seat into the big tournament. The benefit of playing in the two-step events is that they provide a way for you to win an often expensive, Main Event tournament seat at a much lower cost. Chris Moneymaker made the two-step satellite process famous in 2003, the year he won $2.5 million as the WSOP Main Event champion. He started by entering and winning a $39 Step 1 satellite on Pokerstars.com. He followed that win by playing the Step 2 qualifying satellite in which he won his entry into the WSOP Main Event.

This book teaches you how to play live, two-step, sit-and-go satellites to win a seat into a major tournament with a buy-in of $10,000. Your main objective in the first step is to finish first, and your main objective in the second step is to survive until the top two.

> You make your profits in sit-and-go satellites from making heads-up deals.

You don't even have to win the second step to make big money because when you are heads up, you will negotiate a deal to end the match and guarantee yourself a big profit. For this reason, I recommend playing in satellites that allow players to make a deal. Deal making is almost always allowed in live satellites and in online satellites, policies vary depending on which poker site you use.

Both online and live sit-and-go satellites for big-money tournaments are about turning a small-investment into a larger cash return. However, I will show you that playing live satellites is far more lucrative than playing online sit-and-goes.

AN ADAPTABLE SATELLITE STRATEGY

While the strategies and hand examples in this book focus on two-step satellites for big-money events, you can use these strategies to make money from either one-step or two-step satellites for smaller tournaments that cost less to enter. In other words, the strategies in this book are applicable across a wide array of tournament satellites.

The format of the satellites you choose to play could differ from the format you will learn in this book. The Step 2 WSOP qualifier that Chris Moneymaker played was actually a multi-table satellite that had no cap on the number of players signing up. Pokerstars simply handed out one WSOP Main Event seat for every 30 players. You can still apply many of the principles in this book to that type of satellite format, although multi-table satellites aren't ideal, as I explain in the next section.

Another format you will find at some casinos is two-table satellites instead of single-table satellites. You can easily adapt the system in this book to make a lot of money from two-table satellites, which I have done on numerous occasions.

WHY NOT PLAY MULTI-TABLE, BIG-FIELD SATELLITES?

You can win a seat into the World Series of Poker, a World Poker Tour event, or any other big-money tournament in more than one way. One commonly used method is playing large online multi-table satellites that award seats into a main event to a few top finishers. As with the single-table satellite structure that I advocate, playing online multi-table satellites gives you the opportunity to win your way into a big buy-in event very cheaply. You can also play a live multi-table satellite to win your way into the Main Event for the WSOP, WPT, EPT or APPT at the host casino.

But there are some problems with playing multi-table tournaments, whether you play online or live. They can be time consuming, and competing in them is always mentally and physically draining. Many online multi-table satellites are huge and can begin with a few hundred people or sometimes over one thousand players. Large fields can be particularly problematic if you plan on playing in the main event later that day, or even the next day, because you might not be in peak condition. And it can be difficult to finish deep in a large tournament because so many things need to go your way over an extended period of time and against so many opponents. Consequently, it is more difficult to achieve the result you want in large multi-table tournaments.

In addition, there aren't always reliable ways to make deals and profit from playing in multi-table satellites. For example, let's say that you are at the Bellagio in Las Vegas playing in a live multi-table satellite for a main event seat into the WPT Doyle Brunson Five Diamond World Poker Classic. It is close to the end of the tournament, which is down to two tables. There are seventeen players left, and there are twelve main event seats available for the players who finish in the top twelve. After five hours of poker playing, you have only a small chip stack and you want to hedge against getting knocked out and ending up with nothing to show for your time and financial investment.

You want to get some of the players who are currently in a position to win a seat to agree to pay out some cash to you and the other four players who are not currently in a position to win a seat. By accepting their cash, you and the other four players agree to forfeit the tournament. This prevents the chip leaders from getting unlucky and losing their opportunities to win a main event seat when they are so close to it, while letting you and the other short stacks walk away with more cash than you paid to enter this multi-table satellite. The deal certainly makes sense for everyone, doesn't it?

But wait! There's a problem: You'll have to get all the people at both tables to agree to a deal—and that can be difficult. You will look like the ringmaster of a three-ring circus and the distraction you create in trying to explain the deal and get so many people on board will be enough for many players to turn it down. Most players will prefer to just get back to playing and concentrating on the game.

That is why the focus in this book is on teaching you how to win smaller sit-and-goes, particularly single-table satellites, in which you can repeatedly turn a profit.

WHY SINGLE-TABLE SATELLITES ARE IDEAL

I have made a lot of money winning and selling Main Event seats that I won in single-table satellites, or getting paid off to forfeit when I was short-stacked. That's why I can confidently say that my method is the most reliable and profitable strategy you can use to make a profit at single-table satellites.

I recommend single-table tournaments for these five important reasons:

1. TIME

One-table satellites finish quickly. They sometimes finish in as little as two hours, depending on the blind structure and how much time is given for each blind level. If you have traveled to a casino that will be hosting a big tournament and you have given yourself only one or two days to win your way into the main event, single-table satellites are ideal.

2. BANKROLL

The first tournament level is very cheap relative to the amount of money you are looking to make from the whole process. If you can afford to pay for a large number of sit-and-goes and have allotted yourself enough time to play them, you can set yourself up to make a lot of profit.

3. RESULTS

When you play a series of single-table satellites, you'll have a much higher probability of achieving a great result than playing multi-table, big-field satellites. Even after spending an entire day or longer competing in one large tournament, things often don't go your way. You can get unlucky by taking a bad beat, you can go card dead, and sometimes you can make just one poor decision that results in getting knocked out. Suddenly, there goes your entire day with no energy left for playing another one.

Single table satellites only require that you get through nine opponents. In fact, merely getting through eight people will be all you need to do to make a great profit. Therefore, it makes sense to build a good bankroll and to set aside the time to be able to play several single-table satellites.

4. PROFIT

Ultimately, by playing a lot of single-table tournaments, you will have more opportunities to make deals or win multiple seats into a Main Event and sell them. Cash profit is your end goal—and single-table satellites are the best way to reach that goal. You can learn more about how much money you can make in the section titled "A Proven Profit Picture."

5. OPPONENTS

Live single-table satellites often attract a lot of weak players. Whether at the WSOP in Las Vegas or a WPT event, the allure of appearing on TV at a final table and the chance to become the next poker millionaire motivates hundreds of amateur players to make the trip and give it a try. The presence of amateurs is a key determinant in your strategy coming to fruition.

While there are plenty of amateurs playing online, one key difference is that once you sign up for a satellite at a live event, you will have the opportunity to continue playing against the same weak players, who often lose and immediately sign up to play another satellite. This means that if a sit-and-go doesn't go your way, you will be able to play again against the same weak players. Eventually you will come out on top, and sometimes you will even take down a few scores in one day.

Once you learn to play sit-and-go satellites properly—and you will learn these winning strategies in the next few chapters—this process can be extremely lucrative. Just remember that you will need to find enough time to play a few sit-and-goes, and have a sufficient bankroll to get you started.

Now let's take a look at how the two-step satellite system works.

4

A BIRDS-EYE VIEW OF THE TWO-STEP SATELLITE SYSTEM

After reading this book, you not only will understand how to make a profit from playing traditional online sit-and-goes, you will gain a great new way to generate cash from playing satellites for big-money events. These strategies will help make you a more polished tournament player and an expert at creating profits from playing no-limit hold'em.

Here is a look at the satellite structure for which you will be trained:

LEVEL A
10-player single-table
$170 satellite

LEVEL B
10-player single-table
$1,240 satellite

LEVEL C
$10,300 Main Event

This arrangement is designed for a player to be able to win an expensive seat into a no-limit hold'em main event, which costs $10,300, after putting up relatively few dollars. Here's the way it works.

HOW IT WORKS

The winner of the Level A sit-and-go plays for free in the Level B sit-and-go, and if he wins level B, he wins the main event seat. The format and cost structure you see above is the exact same as the one that the WPT used at Niagara Falls, Canada for the 2008 tournament, although the basic structure is the same for any big buy-in tournament in any country.

It starts with ten players who pay $170 to play in the Level A satellite, which creates a prize pool of $1,700. The winner receives a voucher for the Level B satellite, which is valued at $1,240, and the runner up gets a voucher for a free replay at Level A, which is valued at $170. The casino keeps the remaining $290, which is used in part to tip the dealers.

Next, the winners of Level A use their vouchers to play in a Level B satellite. Some of the players in Level B have paid $1,240 to play and some have won their vouchers. The winner of the Level B satellite gets a voucher for the main event valued at $10,300, and the runner up gets a free replay in a Level B satellite, valued at $1,240. Note that the cost of playing each level will vary depending on the cost of the main event seat. For example, the Doyle Brunson Five Diamond World Poker Classic at The Bellagio is a more expensive event, so the satellites cost more. That tournament has a $15,400 buy-in so Level A costs $240 to enter, and Level B costs $1,800.

The key component of this process is that when the match is heads-up in either the Level A or B satellites, the two players can reach an agreement to end the match, based on some financial incentive for each party. The chip leader will usually want to protect his opportunity to win an expensive main event seat by paying his short-stacked opponent to concede, thereby guaranteeing himself his seat and creating profit for the runner-up. The opportunity to strike a deal when a lot of money from the prize pool is on the line, especially in Level B satellites, is a key determinant of the strategies you are about to learn.

KEY TAKEAWAY

Your ultimate goal in the two-step satellite system is negotiating a deal heads-up in Level B. That is when you create profit!

HOW SATELLITE STRATEGY CHANGES FOR LEVEL A AND LEVEL B

Here is an outline of how you will be trained to play for each stage of this satellite process. Notice that the strategies are very different for Level A and Level B:

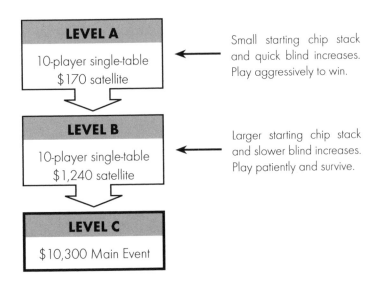

| **LEVEL A** |
| 10-player single-table |
| $170 satellite |

Small starting chip stack and quick blind increases. Play aggressively to win.

| **LEVEL B** |
| 10-player single-table |
| $1,240 satellite |

Larger starting chip stack and slower blind increases. Play patiently and survive.

| **LEVEL C** |
| $10,300 Main Event |

In Level A satellites, you start with very few chips and there are very short periods between blind increases. Frequently this is only ten minutes, which is very quick for a live game. Also, only one prize is awarded, which is a Level B voucher for the winner, although second place wins a free replay in Level A. Therefore, an aggressive winner-take-all approach is best. This doesn't mean that you will move in for all your chips every second hand—you will still pick your spots to get your money in when you are ahead. However, you won't have time to wait to play only premium hands because you can get blinded out that way. With an overly patient approach, you will also surrender too many pots when you are holding the best hand.

In Level B you get more chips and more time between blind increases, which allows you to play more patiently. In addition, your main objective in Level B is to merely survive long enough to place in the top two and negotiate a deal so that you can turn a profit. For this reason, you will find that playing in Level B is a lot like playing in online single-table sit-and-goes, where your main objective is to survive long enough to place in the top three.

YOUR OBJECTIVES FOR LEVEL A AND LEVEL B

Here is an overview of your objectives for each step of this satellite process.

Step 1: Play as many $170 Level A sit-and-goes as you can. You want to win many of these because you want to play a lot of Level B sit-and-goes, which is where you will find the best opportunities to make money. While there is a lot of money to be made playing Level B satellites, you still don't want to buy into them unless you are already significantly in the profit column and you can afford to do so. Therefore, you will want to win as many Level A satellites as you can.

Step 2: Play $1,240 Level B satellites to win multiple main event seats or to negotiate a deal for cash profit. Your objective is to make it to a heads-up match. If you have a chip lead heads-up you can consider making a deal where you pay off your opponent to concede first place to you. If he accepts you can either play in the main event or sell your extra main event seat for cash. Obviously, you would only make an offer that ensures you make more money than you have spent to reach that level B sit-and-go after you sell your extra main event seat. If you are behind in the chip count you can ask your opponent for a deal whereby you get paid off for conceding first place. You would also get a free replay for finishing in second place, which you would use to play another $1,240 satellite and possibly earn more cash.

Step 3: Take your profits from step 2 and either return to step 1 to start the process over again, or remain in step 2 by buying into a Level B sit-and-go. This is a money making cycle that pays for itself. In the next section, you will see a realistic view of how much money you can make over the long term by mastering the poker strategies in this book and playing through this satellite structure numerous times.

5 THE PROVEN PROFIT PICTURE

In business, we look for the most effective route to making a profit. With this basic axiom in mind, let's compare the profit picture for traditional online sit-and-goes with the profit potential of live sit-and-go satellites.

The satellite system I present in this book will enable you to generate long-term cumulative profit growth. Instead of just promising you all kinds of terrific cash profits, I decided to show you how much profit you can make with my satellite method. I will compare the actual profit you make playing sit-and-go satellites with the profits you make playing standard online sit-and-goes. Let's start by looking at the profits you can make playing two-step satellites to win a seat in the Main Event of big-money poker tournament.

THE PROFIT PICTURE FOR SIT-AND-GO SATELLITES

Looking at the profit charts for sit-and-go satellites, you will find that even average players can grow their profits with my sit-and-go method. To show you what kind of profits you can expect from playing satellites, I've built a basic financial model that I will walk you through.

Let's start with a reasonable assumption about how often you will win a Level A sit-and-go satellite. With the approach that I outline in this book, it is fair to assume that you will win on average one out of every five Level A sit-and-goes you play, and the win ratio will be better than that for many readers. Winning Level A after every fifth attempt means that your skills rank on average in the top half of the players at the poker table, which is a conservative assumption.

Now let's look at the average cost of winning a Level B voucher. Since each Level A sit-and-go costs $170, the average cost of winning a Level B voucher will be 5 x $170 = $850. You can see that it is profitable to play Level A sit-and-goes because, even with just run-of-the-mill results, it costs you $850 to win $1,240. You save $390 by playing Level A satellites instead of just buying into Level B.

Let's consider how frequently you can expect to finish in the top two of a Level B sit-and-go and the corresponding financial implications. It is fair to assume that since you are only looking to finish in the top two instead of aiming to win a Level B sit-and-go, you will accomplish this on average one out of every four times you play, although some readers will be able to average a better result than that. Now that we have an expectation of how often you will get paid, let's look at the average prize money you will win, or rather that you will negotiate for when you make it to the top two.

Generally, if two opponents want to end a match and chop a prize pool, they count their chips and let the size of their chip stacks determine the percentage of the prize pool each player gets. For example, if one player has $15,000 in chips, the other player has $5,000 in chips, and there is $1,000 in the prize pool, the chip leader would get three-quarters of the prize money, or $750, since he has three-quarters of the chips in play.

However, you might not want to chop the prize money strictly according to chip count. The caliber of your opponent should influence your decision about how much money to accept. For example, if your opponent is a very tough player, you might consider taking less than your fair share of the prize pool because if you were to play out the match, you could have a difficult time winning. Conversely, if your opponent is a weaker player, you might insist on receiving more than your fair share because you would be agreeing to end a match against an opponent you can probably beat.

In the long run, however, you would probably face an equal number of weak and strong opponents for your heads-up match. A large number of weak players are usually at the table, and all it takes is for one of these players to get lucky and go deep, whereas the fewer good players can finish in the top two more often because they have better skills. Therefore, we'll assume that you're up against an average player heads-up. This means that for the purpose of this analysis, we won't adjust the prize splits according to whether or not we demand more money against a weak opponent or are willing to accept less money against a tough opponent. (Later in the book when I more closely examine how and when to execute a deal, I discuss a concept that I call concession odds. These odds serve as a guide to how much you should deviate from the chip count when assessing the amount of money you would seek when negotiating a deal.)

To figure out an average of how much you will get paid for finishing in the top two, we also have to make an assumption about the relative chip stacks because that factor influences the amount of money you settle for. Assume that in the long run, the average chip ratio is 1 to 1—you and your opponent have the same number of chips. In other words, when you finish in the top two, you probably come out even in the long run among the times you are ahead in chips and the times you are behind in chips, although perhaps you could give a slight edge to having fewer chips due to the low-risk, low-reward style of play you will employ in level B. Also, while the deals that you actually negotiate might not average as high as $5,150, which is half the prize money and the dollar figure associated with a 1 to 1 chip ratio, the occasions in which you win the whole $10,300 prize will make up for it. This will occasionally happen when you beat an opponent who declined to work out a chop.

In short, and to keep this analysis simple, let's assume that on average you win $5,000 when you finish in the top two.

Now that we have all our working assumptions, let's look at the profit you make. You spend an average of $850 (5 x $170 = $850) for every Level B sit-and-go you play. Therefore, after an average of four attempts to finish in the top two in Level B, you will have spent $3,400 (4 x $850 = $3,400) to win $5,000, for a total profit of $1,600. This gives you an excellent 47 percent return on your $3,400 investment (($1,600/$3,400) x 100 = 47 percent).

Even if you have more difficulty finishing in the top two in Level B than most players—that is, on average it takes you 1 out of every 5 times—it would cost you $4,250 (5 x $850 = $4,250) to win $5,000. You would make a $750 profit, which still gives you a nice return on investment of 18 percent. But since you are reading this book and preparing yourself to play Level B sit-and-goes, it is more likely that you will make it to a heads-up match one out of every three or four attempts on average. Clearly there is some amazing profit to be made by learning this process!

Below are tables and charts that map out your cumulative profit after several top two finishes. The tables are separated according to the cost of winning a Level A sit-and-go. For example, the first table shows cumulative profit for a player who averages three attempts to win a Level A sit-and-go, which costs $510 (3 x $170 = $510). The second table shows cumulative profit for a player who averages four attempts to win level A, which costs $680 (4 x $170 = $680), and so forth.

Each table shows the profit you generate after taking into account the average number of attempts it takes you to finish in the top two at Level B. For example, in the first table it costs you $2,040 to win one $5,000 prize, assuming that it takes you an average of four tries to finish in the top two in Level B (4 x $510 = $2,040). The more you play, the more times you earn $2,960 average profit. As you continue in the satellite process, you create larger cumulative profit, which is why the numbers get larger as you move toward the right on the chart.

CUMULATIVE PROFIT FROM BIG-MONEY SATELLITES

Average of 3 attempts to win Level A	Voucher Cost	NUMBER OF TOP 2 FINISHES ($5,000 PAYOUTS) IN LEVEL B							
		1	2	3	4	5	6	7	8
1	$510	$4,490	$8,980	$13,470	$17,960	$22,450	$26,940	$31,430	$35,920
2	$1020	$3,980	$7,960	$11,940	$15,920	$19,900	$23,880	$27,860	$31,840
Avg. # of attempts for a top 2 finish in level B — 3	$1530	$3,470	$6,940	$10,410	$13,880	$17,350	$20,820	$24,290	$27,760
4	$2040	$2,960	$5,920	$8,880	$11,840	$14,800	$17,760	$20,720	$23,680
5	$2550	$2,450	$4,900	$7,350	$9,800	$12,250	$14,700	$17,150	$19,600
6	$3060	$1,940	$3,880	$5,820	$7,760	$9,700	$11,640	$13,580	$15,520

Average of 4 attempts to win Level A	Voucher Cost	NUMBER OF TOP 2 FINISHES ($5,000 PAYOUTS) IN LEVEL B							
		1	2	3	4	5	6	7	8
1	$680	$4,320	$8,640	$12,960	$17,280	$21,600	$25,920	$30,240	$34,560
2	$1360	$3,640	$7,280	$10,920	$14,560	$18,200	$21,840	$25,480	$29,120
Avg. # of attempts for a top 2 finish in level B — 3	$2040	$2,960	$5,920	$8,880	$11,840	$14,800	$17,760	$20,720	$23,680
4	$2720	$2,280	$4,560	$6,840	$9,120	$11,400	$13,680	$15,960	$18,240
5	$3400	$1,600	$3,200	$4,800	$6,400	$8,000	$9,600	$11,200	$12,800
6	$4080	$920	$1,840	$2,760	$3,680	$4,600	$5,520	$6,440	$7,360

Average of 5 attempts to win Level A

	Voucher Cost	NUMBER OF TOP 2 FINISHES ($5,000 PAYOUTS) IN LEVEL B							
		1	2	3	4	5	6	7	8
1	$850	$4,150	$8,300	$12,450	$16,600	$20,750	$24,900	$29,050	$33,200
2	$1700	$3,300	$6,600	$9,900	$13,200	$16,500	$19,800	$23,100	$26,400
3 (Avg. # of attempts for a top 2 finish in level B)	$2550	$2,450	$4,900	$7,350	$9,800	$12,250	$14,700	$17,150	$19,600
4	$3400	$1,600	$3,200	$4,800	$6,400	$8,000	$9,600	$11,200	$12,800
5	$4250	$750	$1,500	$2,250	$3,000	$3,750	$4,500	$5,250	$6,000
6	$5100	-$100	-$200	-$300	-$400	-$500	-$600	-$700	-$800

Average of 6 attempts to win Level A

	Voucher Cost	NUMBER OF TOP 2 FINISHES ($5,000 PAYOUTS) IN LEVEL B							
		1	2	3	4	5	6	7	8
1	$1020	$3,980	$7,960	$11,940	$15,920	$19,900	$23,880	$27,860	$31,840
2	$2040	$2,960	$5,920	$8,880	$11,840	$14,800	$17,760	$20,720	$23,680
3 (Avg. # of attempts for a top 2 finish in level B)	$3060	$1,940	$3,880	$5,820	$7,760	$9,700	$11,640	$13,580	$15,520
4	$4080	$920	$1,840	$2,760	$3,680	$4,600	$5,520	$6,440	$7,360
5	$5100	-$100	-$200	-$300	-$400	-$500	-$600	-$700	-$800
6	$6120	-$1,120	-$2,240	-$3,360	-$4,480	-$5,600	-$6,720	-$7,840	-$8,960

THE PROFIT PICTURE FOR TRADITIONAL ONLINE SIT-AND-GO TOURNAMENTS

The following cumulative profit tables illustrate how much money you can win in the long run in traditional online sit-and-goes while taking into account your skill level. Your skill level is represented in these tables by the average number of times that you cash, which means finishing in the top three. The first table at the top is for players who routinely play online sit-and-goes with a $109 buy-in, where $100 goes into the prize pool and $9 goes to the poker site. In these sit-and-goes there is $900 in the prize pool, where 50 percent ($450) is paid to first place, 30 percent ($270) is paid to second place, and 20 percent ($180) is paid to third place. The average payout for a top-three finish in these tables is $300, which I used to simplify the analysis. I took an average of the top three places paid because, when you finish in the money, you won't win every time, finish second every time, or finish third every time.

Here is how to read and interpret the $100 plus $9 sit-and-go chart. If you are an excellent player who reaches the top three on average every 1.5 times you play, you will make on average $137 profit each time you do so. The more you cash the higher your cumulative profit, which is why the numbers get larger as you move toward the right on the chart. Of course, these numbers get larger by $137 each time you cash, so after cashing ten times, you will have earned $1,370 in profit. Of course, you can play these sit-and-goes many more times and cash far more often than ten times, but I didn't have enough room in this example to illustrate profits after dozens or hundreds of cashes. Nevertheless, you can see that a strong player who knows how to routinely finish in the money can earn excellent profit in the long run playing online sit-and-goes.

Players with above average skills will cash on average every two times they play, and they can earn $820 in profit after ten cashes. Players with average skills will cash on average every 2.5 times they play, and they can earn $280 in profit after ten cashes. Lesser skilled players who take on average three tries or more to cash will lose money in the long run. (You may find this is to be an epiphany for you. Learn from this and ensure that you work hard on your online game so that you can routinely cash more often than once every three tries.)

> **KEY TAKEAWAY**
>
> To make a profit at online sit-and-goes, you must cash more than once in every three tries. Work hard to improve your game and you'll get there.

Of course, the tables for $55 buy-ins and $33 buy-ins are set up the same way as that for the $109 buy-in, and should be read and interpreted the same way.

CUMULATIVE PROFIT FROM ONLINE SIT-AND-GOES

NUMBER OF TOP 3 FINISHES (AVERAGE $300 PAYOUTS)

Cumulative profit from $100+$9 online sit-and-goes

Avg. # of attempts to achieve payout	1	2	3	4	5	6	7	8	9	10
1	$191	$382	$573	$764	$955	$1,146	$1,337	$1,528	$1,719	$1,910
1.5	$137	$274	$411	$548	$685	$822	$959	$1,096	$1,233	$1,370
2	$82	$164	$246	$328	$410	$492	$574	$656	$738	$820
2.5	$28	$56	$84	$112	$140	$168	$196	$224	$252	$280
3	-$27	-$54	-$81	-$108	-$135	-$162	-$189	-$216	-$243	-$270
3.5	-$82	-$164	-$246	-$328	-$410	-$492	-$574	-$656	-$738	-$820
4	-$136	-$272	-$408	-$544	-$680	-$816	-$952	-$1,088	-$1,224	-$1,360

NUMBER OF TOP 3 FINISHES (AVERAGE $150 PAYOUTS)

Cumulative profit from $50+$5 online sit-and-goes

Avg. # of attempts to achieve payout	1	2	3	4	5	6	7	8	9	10
1	$95	$190	$285	$380	$475	$570	$665	$760	$855	$950
1.5	$68	$136	$204	$272	$340	$408	$476	$544	$612	$680
2	$40	$80	$120	$160	$200	$240	$280	$320	$360	$400
2.5	$13	$26	$39	$52	$65	$78	$91	$104	$117	$130
3	-$15	-$30	-$45	-$60	-$75	-$90	-$105	-$120	-$135	-$150
3.5	-$43	-$86	-$129	-$172	-$215	-$258	-$301	-$344	-$387	-$430
4	-$70	-$140	-$210	-$280	-$350	-$420	-$490	-$560	-$630	-$700

Cumulative profit from $30+$3 online sit-and-goes	NUMBER OF TOP 3 FINISHES (AVERAGE $90 PAYOUTS)									
	1	2	3	4	5	6	7	8	9	10
1	$57	$114	$171	$228	$285	$342	$399	$456	$513	$570
1.5	$41	$82	$123	$164	$205	$246	$287	$328	$369	$410
2	$24	$48	$72	$96	$120	$144	$168	$192	$216	$240
2.5	$8	$16	$24	$32	$40	$48	$56	$64	$72	$80
3	-$9	-$18	-$27	-$36	-$45	-$54	-$63	-$72	-$81	-$90
3.5	-$26	-$52	-$78	-$104	-$130	-$156	-$182	-$208	-$234	-$260
4	-$42	-$84	-$126	-$168	-$210	-$252	-$294	-$336	-$378	-$420

Avg. # of attempts to achieve payout

THE BOTTOM LINE

Here is what you can learn from the satellite charts. Look at the third table labeled "Average of 5 Attempts to Win Level A." It shows that a player who wins Level A on average after five tries, and who earns a top-two finish in Level B after an average of three attempts, will have earned a cumulative profit of $19,600 after finishing in the top two for the eighth time. That is an impressive cash profit, especially when you consider that it started with just $170 investments in Level A. Of course, you could continue playing these sit-and-goes and achieve top-two finishes more than eight times (which I have done). These tables show that playing sit-and-go satellites is clearly a profitable venture in the long run, even for poker players with average skills.

Now go back and look at the Online Sit-and-Go Cumulative Profit charts. You will notice that even the $109 buy-in sit-and-goes don't come close to the profit you can make from playing satellites. Even if you consider that you can play multiple tables online at the same time, which speeds up the rate at which you earn profits, you will need hundreds of cashes to earn as much as you can earn in satellites. For example, an online sit-and-go player with better than average skills earns $82 in profit if he cashes on average every two times in a $109 sit-and-go. This player will need to cash 239 times in order to earn the $19,600 that an above average satellite player earns from cashing eight times, assuming he wins Level A after five tries and cashes in Level B after three tries.

Now go back and look at the Online Sit-and-Go Cumulative Profit charts. You will notice that even the $109 buy-in sit-and-goes don't come close to the profit you can make from playing satellites. Furthermore, at the $109 level you are playing against mostly experienced online players and, sometimes, one or two well-known pros. While the investment is smaller compared to a $170 Level A satellite, the difference in skill level more than makes up for the difference in cost. This is true because you will find far weaker opponents playing in live Level A and B satellites than in the $109 online sit-and-go standard tournaments.

You might think that playing even larger online sit-and-goes is the right way to even the investment in our comparison between satellite profits and online sit-and-goes. Think again! Most online poker sites do not run sit-and-goes that cost more than $200 very frequently, and they usually contain highly experienced players.

APPLES AND ORANGES

In reality, comparing Level A and B satellites to online sit-and-goes is like comparing apples to oranges. The formats are different and both you and your opponents have different objectives. You seek a cash profit in online sit-and-goes and you seek a Main Event seat in satellites.

Your time commitment is also quite different. You need to dedicate more time to winning a Level B voucher and to playing out Level B satellites to earn your profits. But despite the greater time commitment and higher absolute cost of satellites, the $10,000 Main Event tournament seat makes the satellite process far more lucrative.

To better understand and master the strategy that I recommend for big money sit-and-go satellites, it is important to first understand the strategy that I propose for traditional online single-table sit-and-goes. Since lower buy-in one-table tournaments are fairly cheap to play online, you can use your online site as a classroom to become more comfortable with single-table events and practice the skills you'll need when you move up to two-step satellites.

The next section teaches you the basic strategies you'll need to win traditional online sit-and-go tournaments.

6 HOW TO PLAY TRADITIONAL ONLINE SINGLE-TABLE SIT-AND-GOES

You can borrow strategies from playing traditional online sit-and-goes to help you accomplish your goals in satellites. For example, the objective of playing a traditional online sit-and-go tournament is to profit from finishing in the top three. Your objective in big-money satellites is to make a profit by finishing in the top two. You can practice your top-three-finish skills in online tournaments, and then easily adapt them to your satellite skills.

HOW YOU CAN USE ONLINE SIT AND GOES TO PRACTICE FOR BIG-MONEY SATELLITES

The most important skills you need to develop in playing online sit-and-goes are patience and risk management. You can draw on these strategies to achieve your goals in Level B satellites. Since you will often need to play the early and late stages of Level B satellites conservatively, learning to play patiently and manage your risk taking will greatly improve your chances of reaching your ultimate objective in Level B— playing heads-up to win a seat in a big-money tournament.

In addition, you will learn to more consistently and frequently turn a profit when you play an ordinary online single-table sit-and-go.

THE STYLE OF PLAY THAT WILL GET YOU THERE

A consistent and low-risk style of play will enable you to routinely finish in the money in traditional online sit-and-goes. The main reason for playing conservatively is that it works well against the aggressive playing style of most online players. For example, when you make a preflop raise, you often get callers who want to take a look at the flop. They just can't help themselves!

Therefore, you don't want to get too carried away with stealing blinds unless you are short-stacked and you desperately need chips. Why? Because your opponents usually will call you. If you raise in position preflop and then bet the flop, a caller will often try to bluff you with a check-raise. Or someone with second pair or a small pocket pair will call your raise hoping that you have made a continuation bet with nothing. In fact, when you're playing the flop in any situation online, an opponent usually will bet if you check-bet.

In short, online players don't often believe their opponents are holding a strong hand and they always pounce on perceived weakness.

Keeping these facts in mind when you play online will serve as a solid guide for how to play your hands in most situations. Since your opponents will usually play aggressively, it follows that the best strategy to offset their aggressiveness is to wait for a strong hand with which to get paid off, unless you are short-stacked and are forced to play marginal hands.

> **KEY TAKEAWAY**
>
> Online players often doubt their opponents have solid hands.
> If you wait patiently, you can trap them with your strong hands.

ONLINE SIT-AND-GO TOURNAMENT STRUCTURE

A standard nine-player, online single-table sit-and-go has friendly blind levels, which usually start at around $15/$30 or $20/$40. Starting chip stacks are usually between forty and sixty times the big blind, so they can vary from $1,200 to $1,800, depending on which site you play. Also, you are often given five or six minutes per round before the blinds increase. While five minutes might seem short, remember that you see far more hands when playing online than in a live game because of the speed with which hands are dealt and played out. This means that if you play at a slow pace and show some patience, you will eventually be rewarded with strong hands.

ONLINE SIT-AND-GO OBJECTIVE AND STRATEGY

Your objective in online sit-and-goes is to finish in the money, which is the top three. Each time you do so, you make a profit on your investment, which is your buy-in. Since you have ample time to wait patiently for strong hands in online sit-and-goes, an effective approach is to spend the majority of your time sitting back and letting your opponents play against each other. You want your opponents to cripple each other's chip stacks and knock each other out because each time that happens, it brings you closer to finishing in the top three.

In an online sit-and-go, very often all it takes to finish in the money is to win one or two good-sized pots. Therefore, the most important parts of your job are the following:

1. **Wait patiently for strong hands**

2. **Don't waste chips by**
   a. Trying to steal too many blinds
   b. Calling large raises preflop with marginal and trash hands just to see if you hit a big flop. Note the odds of flopping two pair with each of your hole cards is about 48 to 1, and the odds of flopping three of a kind with one of your hole cards is about 73 to 1.
   c. Frequently making continuation bets in multiway pots. You should mostly make continuation bets when you are heads up.

3. **Avoid playing coin flips in big pots**
   Consider this a warning against calling all-in bets with small pocket pairs, unless you are very short-stacked and need to win a coin flip just to avoid getting blinded out.

4. **Avoid playing drawing hands**
   Unless an opponent bets very small and you are getting irresistible pot odds, never chase cards. Also, don't get into the habit of raising with your draws since as you now know, your opponents don't often fold, which takes away much of the value of making that play.

MAKING STRATEGIC FOLDS

Here's a very important rule of thumb in almost any sit-and-go format: You don't want to get knocked out before the weaker players get knocked out. You want to stick around long enough for your opponents to make a big mistake so that you can win their chips. This means that you will need to make a tough fold in a few situations. Here are some examples of those situations.

1. WHEN AN OPPONENT RAISES BEFORE THE FLOP

Suppose the blinds are $15/$30 and all nine players are still in the tournament. You still have your starting chip stack of $1,500, and you are in the cutoff position with A♥ Q♥. A player in early position raises to $90 and another player reraises to $250.

You need to fold here because there is a very good chance your hand is beaten. Since it is very early in the sit-and-go and you still have all your chips, there is little reason to get involved in a war with a solid but still vulnerable hand like A-Q. Even if you decide to call the reraise, you don't know how strong the early position raiser is. If he comes over the top, you couldn't call because you could be up against A-K, pocket aces, kings or queens, so you would have wasted $250.

If you think that shoving all-in is a good play because only someone with a monster hand like pocket aces or kings could call, think again! Online players will call early all-in bets with surprisingly weak hands like pocket tens or nines, which would put you in a coin flip situation. Of course, they will also call with A-K.

Don't gamble your sit-and-go away by getting it all-in early with a hand like A-Q. Instead, wait patiently for an opportunity to win a big pot in a situation where you are in control of the hand.

2. WHEN AN OVERCARD COMES ON THE FLOP

The blinds are $25/$50 and seven players remain in the tournament. Players started with $1,500, so the average chip stack is about $1,930. You have $1,475, and you are in middle position with pocket tens. You make a small raise to $120 hoping to push most players out of the hand so that you can play a small heads-up pot, probably against the player in the big blind. You think that the big blind will call since it is only costing him another $70 to see a flop and he has been playing somewhat loose.

SITUATION

Blinds/Antes: $25/$50
You Have: 10♣ 10♦
Money in the Pot: $195
Number of Players: 6

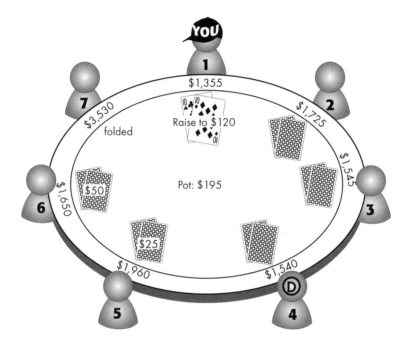

Let's elaborate on why you are making such a small raise. Although you probably have the best starting hand, you want to avoid losing a big pot this early in the tournament in case you get called and have to play a flop. Therefore, you want to keep the pot small both preflop and after the flop. You are hoping that only the big blind calls to look at the flop with two trash cards, that he misses the flop pretty badly, and that you can take it down with a small continuation bet of about $160.

The reason you should keep the pot small is that playing pocket tens after the flop is quite risky. If you look at the table in Appendix B, you will see that there is about a 70 percent chance of at least one overcard hitting the flop when you have pocket tens. If an overcard comes on the flop, you must be prepared to fold if your opponent bets into you, or if he raises your bet. Even if the flop is Q♠ 8♦ 5♥, for example, if you suspect that your opponent has only made a pair of eights, you will likely have to risk a large portion of your chips to find out if your hand is winning. You shouldn't take on substantial risk in such a precarious position, even against a loose player.

Another reason your small preflop raise makes sense is that it ensures that you won't lose a lot of money if you get reraised. You would fold if an opponent reraised your bet at this relatively early stage of the tournament.

As it turns out, only the big blind calls. He has $1,580 chips left. You are playing the hand heads up. The flop comes K♦ 2♥ 5♥, making one overcard on board. He checks. You make a solid but not-too-crazy continuation bet of $175 into a pot of $265. The big blind raises to $450.

SITUATION

Blinds/Antes:	$25/$50
You Have:	10♣ 10♦
The Board:	K♦ 2♥ 5♥
Money in the Pot:	$820
Bet for You to Call:	$275
Number of Players:	2

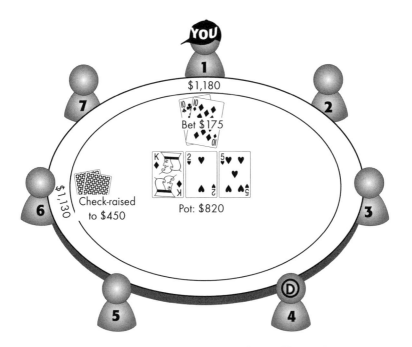

Even though his check-raise is only about 2.5 times your bet and you are getting very enticing pot odds of 3 to 1 on your money to call, folding is the best play here. You don't want to waste so many chips with a vulnerable hand like second pair. Your opponent could have a pair of kings and you are not willing to risk a ton of chips just to satisfy your curiosity. Also, if you move in to push him off a possible draw with a hand like 6♥ 4♥, he might call anyway because he would have a lot of outs (12) to make a straight or flush. In that case, you would have all your chips on the line with only a tiny mathematical edge, which isn't good enough this early in the sit-and-go.

Don't feel compelled to call his check-raise, or to reraise him, just because you have already invested some of your chips in the pot. Even though you spent $295 in the hand and your chip stack is down to $1,180, the blinds aren't that big yet. You still have plenty of time to sit back and wait for an opportunity to win a nice pot and maybe even double up with a strong hand.

Unless you are playing a short stack, wait for opportunities to get your money in when you believe you are ahead.

3. WHEN YOU HAVE A SOLID STARTING HAND AGAINST A BIG RAISE

The blinds are $100/$200 and five players remain in the tournament. The average chip stack is $2,700 and you have $2,550. You are on the button with pocket jacks. The chip leader raises under the gun to $500. He is an active and loose player with $4,580 in chips. The short stack at the table moves in for $1,600. She has been relatively patient and hasn't been shoving at every opportunity. The action is on you.

SITUATION

Blinds/Antes: $100/$200
You Have: J♠ J♣
Money in the Pot: $2,400
Bet for You to Call: $1,600
Number of Players: 5

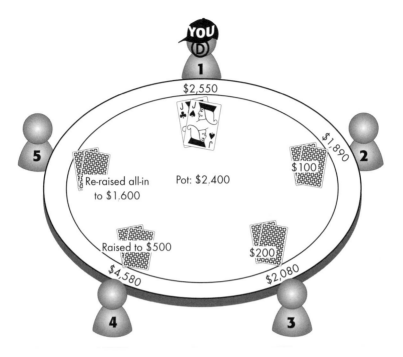

Folding is your best play here. It is possible that the short stack moved in with a marginal hand like A-9 or a smaller pair like eights or nines because she thinks the raiser has nothing. However, she could just as easily be holding hands like A-K, A-Q, K-Q or even A-A, K-K and Q-Q.

You aren't short stacked, so you aren't desperate enough to risk almost two thirds of your chips in a coin flip. If you call with your pocket jacks, the big stack folds, and you lose a showdown against the short stack, you would be left with just $950. That makes it very risky for you to go to war with the reraiser. More importantly, you are the player who is guessing instead of being the player who is controlling the hand by putting his opponents to a decision. Whenever possible you should avoid risking most of your chips at times like this. In addition, if you decide to come over the top, you can't just assume that the chip leader will fold. His presence behind you makes this situation a little more dangerous. Pocket jacks is not a strong hand in a three-way pot, unless you are up against smaller pairs.

You might actually put the short-stack reraiser on a strong hand because she should recognize that the raiser is a loose player with more than enough chips to call to try to knock her out. It's only $1,100 more for the chip leader to call so, with $2,400 in the pot, he's getting better than 2 to 1 on his money. With $4,580 left, he would still have a very slight chip lead if he lost the hand, so he would have to be holding one of the weakest starting hands in hold'em to fold.

Here is another very important factor you need to consider in this hand. By folding you could end up in a pretty nice spot because you might get to see a player eliminated. If the chip leader calls and eliminates the short stack, you would be on the bubble (only one player left to be eliminated before making the money). And you would have a chip stack that isn't in bad shape relative to the size of the blinds. All you would need to do to finish in the money case is wait for one more player to get knocked out.

Remember that in standard sit-and-goes, your objective is to survive and finish in the money. Therefore, you can often benefit by folding and letting your opponents knock each other out.

As it turns out, the big stack calls after you fold and he shows A♦ 10♥. The short stack turns over Q♥ Q♣. The big stack spikes an ace on the flop and wins the hand. You are one step closer to making a profit in this sit-and-go!

HOW TO PLAY THE END GAME

The late stage of a sit-and-go is called the end game. When blinds and antes are very high, there is a lot of pressure on short-stacked players to double up before they run out of chips.

One or two players usually have large chip stacks at this point in the sit-and-go.

WHEN YOU HAVE A LOT OF CHIPS

If you have a lot of chips with only four or five players left, sit back and conserve your chips—let other players take on risk by calling with marginal hands in an effort to knock out the short stacks. Always remember that your objective is to survive long enough to make a profit with a top-three finish. You mustn't take on a lot of risk in an effort to bully your way to first place.

Here's another pointer when you have a lot of chips and you are getting into the later stages of the sit-and-go. Be especially wary of playing a very big pot, one that is more than one quarter of your chips, without having a very strong hand. Instead, try stealing some blinds with minimum raises, which means making a bet that is double the big blind, if you want to pick up some insurance chips. That way, you won't lose a lot if someone reraises and you have to fold.

A minimum raise will seem oddly small to some of your opponents and they might interpret your raise to mean that you are looking for action with a powerful hand. With these types of raises you can successfully prevent your opponents from winning the blinds without risking a lot of chips.

WHEN YOU HAVE A SHORT STACK

When you are getting short-stacked, things become more complicated because it is you that your opponents are looking to pick off. Being a short stack really just comes down to getting your money in with decent hands that aren't often dominated before you get blinded out. These plays include open shoving with pocket pairs, suited connectors, one-and two-gappers, and any ace if the table is short-handed. If you are short-stacked and there are six or more players at your table, avoid moving in with a weak ace like A-6 because an opponent who also has an ace but with a bigger kicker could call you. In that case, you would be about a 3 to 1 underdog.

Fold equity is also important for you to take advantage of as a short stack. This means that you should rarely move in with a marginal hand after an opponent has already opened the pot and it wouldn't cost him a lot to call you. In other words, any time you push with a marginal hand, you want opponents to fold. Therefore, avoid situations where you think they will probably call you.

One exception to this general rule is when you are desperately short stacked; that is, when you have less than five big blinds left. In that case, you may need to move in with any hand that gives you a decent chance to win a pot. Why? Because you no longer have enough chips to make opponents fold if you move in. With so few chips left, you are at risk of getting blinded out, especially if there are antes to pay. The starting hands you need to play can be as weak as Q-8, J-4 or 10-6 suited. If someone with a weak ace such as A-5 calls, you will have a decent chance of doubling up with your queen-high or jack-high hand, since you would be less than a 2 to 1 underdog.

Another important point to know when playing a short stack in online single-table sit-and-goes is that you should try to fold frequently when you are on the bubble. If two opponents are going after each other in a very big pot, get out of the way almost every time unless you are holding pocket aces or kings. That way, you might be able to squeak into the money and turn a profit even with very few chips left. While you will still need to move in a few times in order to steal some blinds, you should space out your plays. You want your opponents to think that you are trying to wait for a good hand with which to push, which should increase your chances of winning the blinds uncontested. Another reason is to allow your opponents to make mistakes by playing at each other.

Now that we've discussed how to play standard online sit-and-goes, let's move right along to playing Level A in sit-and-go satellites to win a seat in a major tournament.

7 HOW TO PLAY LEVEL A SIT-AND-GO SATELLITES

Your main objective in Level A sit-and-goes is to win. You are not looking to make a deal, so chip accumulation is the most effective strategy. The blinds increase fast in Level A satellites, usually every ten or fifteen minutes and you have only $1,200 in starting chips. Of course, the amount of starting chips and length of time between blind increases can vary significantly depending on the particular main event you choose to satellite into. However, the basic structure you learn here will serve as a guide to making money from virtually any one or two-table satellite format.

The basic format starts with a cheap, quick, small-stack satellite (Level A) followed by a more expensive, slightly longer and slightly deeper-stacked satellite (Level B).

THE LEVEL A BLIND STRUCTURE

Here is the Level A blind structure. The first level is $25/$50, followed by $50/$100, $100/$200, $100/$200 with $25 ante, $150/$300 with $50 ante, $200/$400 with $75 ante, $300/$600 with $100 ante, and so on. Notice that you are not afforded the benefit of a few small starting blind levels such as

$10/$20, $15/$30 and $20/$40 like you find in most online sit-and-goes.

In Level A sit-and-go satellites, the rising blinds start to wear away at players' chip stacks much quicker. For example, one preflop raise in just the second blind level could cost more than 25 percent of a player's chip stack. Therefore, if he gets involved in a pot, it might be for all his chips. This gives a significant advantage to the raiser since players need a better hand to call with than they do to raise with.

PLAY AGGRESSIVELY TO WIN CHIPS EARLY

You need to accumulate chips early to avoid becoming short-stacked. If you become short-stacked, you are usually forced to bet all your chips with a marginal hand against opponents who have a lot more chips than you and are likely to call you. If you play too tight, you can become a short stack by just the second or third blind level. Therefore, you need to play aggressively, getting involved in any situation that gives you a good chance to win a pot.

Aggressive poker is usually winning poker in Level A sit-and-goes. It becomes difficult to do battle when you are the one forced to make a call that costs a large portion of your chip stack, especially if you are just hoping to pair one of your hole cards on the flop. Aggressive players with chips have an edge—try to gain that edge in the first level by accumulating chips. You will then have the choice to keep playing aggressively or to sit back a little during the subsequent blind levels and wait to pick off the short stacks.

> **KEY TAKEAWAY**
>
> Blinds increase fast and you start with a small chip stack, so try to win chips early with aggressive play to avoid becoming a short stack.

PLAY A VARIATION OF SMALL-POT POKER

You have leeway to gamble in the first blind level because you can make moves and be the aggressor in numerous hands without it costing you a large portion of your chip stack. This is an important part of aggressive play in Level A sit-and-goes. You want to win a lot of pots but you don't want to risk a ton of chips in any one hand. For example, when the blinds are $25/$50, a preflop raise to $150 followed by a continuation bet of $200 doesn't cripple you if an opponent hits the flop, plays back at you and you are forced to fold. However, you will still take the pot down after the flop a lot of the time. This is the foundation of an effective style called small pot poker.

When the blinds start to get very high, $100/$200 with $25 antes or higher, your preflop raises must be smaller. For your opponents, getting involved in one pot might mean risking all their chips, so it will still take a pretty good hand for them to call even a small raise. Meanwhile, it won't cost you a lot to apply pressure on them.

For example, let's say that the blinds are $100/$200 and you have $2,500 in chips in middle position. A tight player is in the big blind with $1,400 behind. If you decide to steal the pot, you can accomplish this by raising to $500 instead of making the typical raise of three or four times the big blind. You would be putting him to a decision for 21 percent of his remaining chips ($300 more for him to call with $1,400 behind), and he will likely think that if he gets involved, his tournament life will be on the line. While you would also be risking 20 percent of your chips, you would be giving yourself a chance to win the pot right there.

In fact, if the player in the big blind is very tight, you might be able to steal the pot with a minimum raise to $400, assuming nobody limped in front of you. Raising a small amount also serves to conserve your chips when you get called and you need to make a continuation bet—small preflop raises help keep the pot small after the flop. If you try to take it down after the flop, you won't need to bet big, and if your opponent fights back you won't be surrendering a ton of chips if you fold.

Notice the difference between applying pressure and being the one who is challenged with making a call. When someone raises your blind and you have two unpaired hole cards you only have about a 32 percent chance of hitting the flop. For that reason, you will find a lot of amateur players move in preflop without a strong hand when an aggressive player raises their blind. Since they don't know how to play a hand like A♦ 6♣ after the flop, they will just go all-in and hope their opponents can't call. The reason this can be good is that you eventually will be dealt a strong starting hand like A-K, A-Q or a pocket pair such as tens or better. As an aggressive player you will force your opponents to make mistakes against you when you finally hold strong hands—and you will be able to win big pots.

That is precisely why small-pot poker is an effective style. Your persistently active and aggressive style will prevent opponents from knowing how strong your hand is and they will pay you off. Meanwhile, your moderate betting amounts will ensure that you don't get knocked out of the tournament quickly if your opponents hit the flop big. You will stick around long enough for the weaker players to pay you off and build your chip stack.

Notice that I called this section a variation of small-pot poker. Normally in a larger multi-table tournament, aggressive players using small pot strategy will want to avoid getting all their chips in without a big hand early in the tournament. They believe they don't need to risk getting knocked out of a tournament early when they can succeed by outplaying their weaker opponents, and they want to make sure they hang around long enough to do that. However, being unwilling to risk all your chips makes more sense for Level B satellites than it does for Level A satellites because in Level B satellites, the time between blind increases is longer and starting chip stacks are deeper.

Always keep in mind that Level A is a short stacked sit-and-go where winning is the only acceptable outcome. You will not get many opportunities to hold strong cards. You will play a variation of small pot poker in Level A because you will be willing to risk all your chips on any hand that you believe is winning preflop or after the flop, even if it isn't a monster. In fact, be prepared to aggressively play any hand that you think gives you a chance to win a big pot, including a big draw. Your aggressive play will eventually cause some of your opponents to make mistakes and play back at you with weaker hands like 3-3 when you are holding 9-9; or with hands like second or third pair when you are holding top pair after the flop.

To sum up, when you don't have a hand, play aggressively but try to keep the pot small. When you are holding a solid hand, be willing to risk all your chips.

KEY TAKEAWAY

Use a variation of aggressive small-pot poker to accumulate chips. Only risk a lot of chips in a big pot when you have a solid hand.

PLAY A WIDE RANGE OF HANDS

During the first blind level, other players will be waiting around for big pairs, A-K, A-Q and A-J, while you will be raising with a wider range of hands: A-K all the way down to A-9, K-Q, K-J, K-10, Q-J, Q-10, any pocket pair, and low suited connectors (if tight players are in the blinds). If you have raised the last two or three consecutive hands, you can consider limping in with some of the hands listed above, just to change gears a little. In general, if you are playing a pot heads-up and you hit any piece of the board, play it aggressively unless your opponent convinces you that he has you beaten. Remember to bet small and avoid risking your whole tournament with a marginal hand when you aren't confident you are winning.

Never limp in with pocket pairs of nines or higher. These hands are very strong in any short-stacked sit-and-go. You don't want to waste them by limping in and playing a four or five-way pot because, unless you flop a set, you won't know where you're at when the flop comes out. One exception to this rule is when you are on the button or in the small blind with pocket aces, kings or queens and everyone folds around to you preflop. In these cases, you can look to disguise the strength of your starting hand by limping in. Hopefully you can take down a big pot from someone who flops top pair, second pair or maybe a draw when you are holding an overpair.

If you limp in and a player raises behind you preflop, feel free to reraise and even go all-in with these big pairs. Alternatively, you can smooth call a preflop raise to disguise the strength of your hand and take down a big pot if your opponent flops top pair or if he has an overpair to the board that is lower than yours. In a Level A satellite, you needn't worry about an opponent cracking your big pair, assuming there are only two or three of you playing a flop. In a raised pot, as long as there are no overcards on board, be willing to risk all your chips after the flop with a big overpair.

PLAYING A MARGINAL HAND DURING THE FIRST BLIND LEVEL

Here is an example of playing a hand in the first blind level with one of the aforementioned starting hands. You are on the button with A♠ 9♠ at a ten-handed table. The blinds are $25/$50 and you have $1,200 in chips. A seemingly weak-tight player raises to $150 under the gun, and everyone folds around to you. You believe he is weak-tight because in the first hand of the sit-and-go, he limp-folded on the button after the big blind made a silly minimum raise to $100, and after four players had limp-called the raise. It was only $50 more for him to call the $550 pot, so he was getting 11 to 1 on his money, yet he folded a hand with which he initially wanted to see a flop. Apparently, he is new to the sit-and-go events and doesn't know what he is doing.

SITUATION

Blinds/Antes: $25/$50
You Have: A♠ 9♠
Money in the Pot: $225
Bet for You to Call: $150
Number of Players: 4

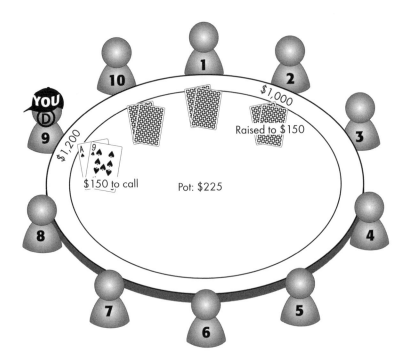

You want to respect your opponent's under-the-gun raise, so you put him on a range of hands such as a big ace, a pocket pair from nines up to kings, or maybe K-Q or K-J. You don't necessarily put him on pocket aces right away because the odds that he is holding that hand when you are holding an ace are more than 20 to 1.

You decide to call for these reasons: Since he is an inexperienced player you think you can outplay him if he misses the flop, and you have position on him. You don't want to reraise here because you would be committing too many chips with a marginal hand without a lot of information about your opponent's hand. In other words, you couldn't call if he came over the top.

The flop is 8♠ 5♣ 4♥. Your opponent is first to act and he checks. You completely missed the flop but you think you might have a chance to win the pot with a bet right here. Since he checked, you suspect that he has two overcards such as A-K, A-Q, A-J, K-Q or K-J. It would be somewhat of a tricky play for him to check-raise or, especially, check-call with an overpair in this spot; and since you consider him to be a novice, you decide that he most likely doesn't have that play in his repertoire.

There is $375 in the pot and you bet $225 hoping your opponent folds. He takes his time, and hesitantly calls. While he could have pocket sevens or sixes and is playing a pair with a gutshot straight draw carefully, it is quite possible that he is overvaluing two overcards like A-K or A-Q and is sticking around because he is unable to let go of a hand like that. If he had pocket tens he probably would have bet out, and with A-8 he would either have bet or check-raised you.

The turn card is the 6♠, so the board is 8♠ 5♣ 4♥ 6♠. Unless your opponent happens to be holding pocket sevens, this is a good card for you because you have a flush draw and a gutshot straight draw. You have twelve outs, nine spades and three sevens, to make a very big hand. Perhaps even more importantly, if your opponent has two overcards, this turn card should scare him, as he might think that you have at least a pair or maybe a straight. He checks.

SITUATION

Blinds/Antes: $25/$50
You Have: A♠ 9♠
The Board: 8♠ 5♣ 4♥ 6♠
Money in the Pot: $825
Number of Players: 2

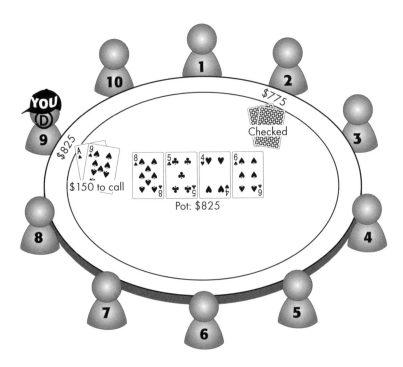

You need to bet here because his checks on both the flop and turn indicate that he is holding a weak hand against this flop and would likely fold. Even if you are wrong and he calls your bet with a set, you would have up to nine outs to make a flush, plus another three outs (three sevens) to make a 9-high straight, so you would still have about a 1 in 3 chance to win the hand with one card to come. If he has made a straight with pocket sevens, you would have nine outs to make a flush, assuming that he isn't holding the 7♠, plus another two outs (two sevens) to make a straight and chop the pot with your opponent.

You move in for your remaining $825 and he folds. You win a $1,650 pot and take an early lead in the sit-and-go.

The key lesson in this hand is that when you are in position against a tight player, especially one that is inexperienced, get involved in hands against him and outplay him after the flop.

PLAYING MARGINAL HANDS AFTER THE FIRST BLIND LEVEL

As players start to get knocked out after the first blind level, you can open up your range of starting hands a little more. You can play A-K down to A-7, K-Q and further down to K-8, Q-J, Q-10, Q-9, any pocket pair, and low suited connectors. By attempting to steal pots and playing a wide range of hands aggressively, you will eventually get paid off by someone who thinks you are bluffing when you actually have caught a strong hand.

During the first blind level, you don't usually want to play for all your chips after the flop without a strong hand, but be aware that after the first level has ended, many players like to move in with a draw against an aggressive player. Moving in with only a drawing hand is one way they may choose to play back at the aggressor while having some outs to win if he calls. Therefore, after the first blind level, you may need to call someone down in a big pot with top pair/weak kicker or, sometimes, even with second pair if you think strongly that they are on a move or are making a semi-bluff.

PICKING OFF SHORT STACKS

Your objective in the first $25/$50 blind level is to accumulate a chip stack of $1,800-$2,000. This gives you a nice buffer against the $50/$100 blinds in the second level and allows you to keep playing aggressively. You will also use your chip stack to start scooping up the short stacks after the first blind level. At $50/$100, you can start calling short stacks that move in preflop for roughly $700 or less. Since you will have them covered and you still wouldn't be crippled if you lost the hand, you should gamble and try to take them out. As a rule of thumb for how much of your chip stack you should be willing to risk, make sure you don't call off more than one third of your chips. Look for coin flips or, preferably, situations in which you are slightly ahead (for example, A-J versus K-Q or 7-7 versus A-9). Hopefully, you will get lucky and catch someone when you are holding a dominating hand (for example, A-J versus A-8).

The hands you will want to play to try to pick off the short stacks are pocket pairs of sevens or higher, an ace with a 10 kicker or higher, K-Q, K-J, and Q-J. The purpose of playing king-high and queen-high hands is to catch someone who moves in with a very weak hand. Even if you are wrong and you only have live cards against an opponent who has a weak ace, you will still have a good chance to win a nice pot and eliminate a player. Meanwhile, losing the pot will not cripple you.

This is a very different type of approach than what you would use early in a deeper stacked tournament. Even though it is fair to assume for any type of sit-and-go that when a short stack moves in, he doesn't usually have a strong hand, you should be less willing to gamble early in a long, deep-stack tournament. The reason is you will have more time to rely on your skill instead of luck to win chips. By comparison, after you start to accumulate chips in a Level A satellite, be willing to risk getting your money in when you are behind once in a while. Just make sure it doesn't cost you more than one third of your chips to play your hand. Remember that in this sit-and-go, your objective is to win and not just survive, so you need the extra chips.

CALLING A SHORT STACK'S ALL-IN BET

Here is an example of calling a short stack's all-in bet. Let's say that you are in the second blind level ($50/$100), you are sitting in the big blind with $1,700, and you are holding K-J offsuit. One player with $1,900 in chips limps in from middle position and a short stack in the cutoff moves in for $600. The button and small blind fold. The action is on you.

SITUATION

Blinds/Antes: $50/$100
You Have: K♦ J♣
Money in the Pot: $850
Number of Players: 3

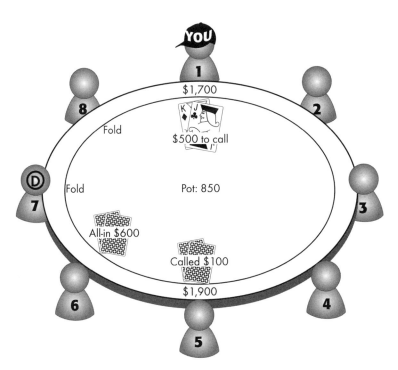

With $850 in the pot, it is costing you another $500 to call, so you are getting 1.7 to 1 on your money. You are only behind by about 1.4 to 1 if he has an ace with a 10-kicker or lower, so it looks like you are getting a good price to call and you can afford to gamble. If he has A-Q you would need about 1.7 to 1 on your money to call, so again you would be getting the right price. He could also have just a low pair, in which case you would be getting a great price to call because it would be a coin toss for you to win, and you would only need even money. Also, there is a chance that your hand is actually winning. He could be making a move with a hand you are beating like J-10, 9-8 or 8-6 suited since nobody showed strength in front of him.

Of course, he might have you dominated with a hand like A-K, A-J or K-Q, but that is a risk you should be willing to take. Since you have the chips to gamble and since you need to accumulate chips to win, you decide to go ahead and play your hand in this situation. Even if you lose, you would still have your original $1,200 starting stack left, which is enough for you to compete.

The only decision left is whether to isolate the short stack by moving in and pushing the limper in Seat 5 out of the hand, or to just call and see if the limper comes over the top, which would indicate that he is probably sandbagging with a powerful hand. The reason you want to consider isolating the short stack is that your hand stands a greater chance of winning when you play it heads-up, because the greater the number of players who look at the flop, the less the likelihood of even the strongest starting hand winning.

Here is how to think about this. If you just call the short stack's all-in bet, you would be priced in to call an all-in reraise by the limper, so you might as well just move in. Let's look at the math. The limper has you covered. If he pushes after you call the $600, you would be getting better than 2.5 to 1 on your money ($3,050 in the pot ÷ $1,200 in chips you have left). If he has a pocket pair of queens or lower, you would be getting the right price to call. At 2.5 to 1, you would almost be getting a good enough price to risk being dominated by a hand like A-K, so you would call. Therefore, you decide to put the pressure on the limper and move in. By reraising you will likely prevent him from looking at the flop with a speculative hand or with a medium-strength hand such as pocket eights.

As it turns out, the limper in Seat 5 folds and the short stack turns over A♥ 2♣. To your surprise, you flop trip jacks. You eliminate the short stack and grow your chip stack to $2,550. You are now set up to continue dominating the table and win the sit-and-go.

WHEN AN OPPONENT PLAYS BACK AT YOU

When you are the aggressor at your table, some players might start moving in on you preflop in the middle or later stages, because they don't know any other way to deal with you. They will just hope that you are holding a hand that is so weak that you have to fold. I like to call these moves "push and pray." When your opponents move in, they hope you won't call, and they will implore the poker gods to allow them to win if you do call. Be sure to feel out your opponents when they move in because their hands will sometimes be weaker than you think.

Here is one of those situations that I recall during a WPT Level A sit-and-go that I won at Niagara Falls, Canada. The blinds were $50/$100 and there were seven players left. I had $2,225 in chips and I raised preflop to $300 in late position with A-7 offsuit after the player sitting on my right had limped in. The player in the big blind moved in for $1,600, and the limper folded, so we were heads-up when the action came back on me.

Just two hands earlier this player had moved in on me after I raised with Q-J offsuit. After I folded my Q-J, he showed A-8 offsuit as if it were a monster hand. He was trying to tell me that he plays strong hands in big pots and that I should fold if he pushes on me again. I felt fortunate that he showed me his hand because I learned something about his game. It seemed that he overvalued what was really just a marginal hand. It's not like he showed me pocket kings, which might indicate that he only pushes with very powerful hands. This time, it felt like he might be pushing with king-high or worse, since he just learned that I was capable of folding. Also, my gut was telling me that it was too coincidental for him to have me beaten with a bigger ace in this spot.

Despite his very large bet, I didn't want to just fold immediately. I took my time to think it through. I thought his bet was so big that it was unlikely he was holding a monster hand like kings or queens, since he would want action with those hands. Why not reraise to just $900? It looked like he was holding a hand that couldn't withstand action after the flop. Knowing that there are a lot of weak players at these satellites who will make mistakes, I thought it was very possible that he was on a resteal with a very weak hand and that I had an opportunity to take a commanding chip lead at the table.

One approach I sometimes like to use to get information out of an opponent is to start counting and stacking my chips to make it look like I'm going to call. After I do that, I'll glance at him to see if he seems nervous. If he does seem nervous, I consider calling. In this case, after I started to count out a stack of $1,300, I noticed my opponent's neck stiffened up and he looked a little pale. He seemed uncomfortable, so I decided to call. He turned over 10-9 offsuit. My A-7 held up, I eliminated a player, and became a big chip leader in a sit-and-go that I eventually won.

Here is another example of how to think through a situation when an opponent plays back at you. The blinds are $100/$200 and there are six players left. You have $2,500 in chips and you are sitting in the cutoff seat holding K♦ 9♣. There are no limpers in front of you and the two players in the blinds have been playing moderately tight. You raise to $550 hoping to steal the blinds. The player to your left sitting on the button goes all-in for $1,400. The blinds fold and you are heads-up.

The button raiser is getting short-stacked and he needs to play a pot to win some chips. You have been pushing the action at the table, so your opponents don't need a really big hand to play back at you; therefore, you don't put him on a monster like a big pair. However, it seems that this particular opponent has been waiting patiently for a solid hand and your K-9 offsuit is likely beaten. Still, you don't want to just muck your hand right away. You need to evaluate how much it is costing you to make the call compared to what is in the pot. There is $2,250 in the pot and it will cost you another $850 to call, which gives you about 2.5 to 1 on your money.

WHAT TYPE OF HAND MIGHT YOUR OPPONENT BE HOLDING?

You start to consider the range of hands you could be up against. Against A-Q, A-J or A-10 you would be behind by about 1.7 to 1. Against an ace with a kicker lower than a 9, you would only be behind by about 1.4 to 1. You are clearly getting a great price to call if he is holding any ace other than A-K. If he has pocket tens, jacks or queens, you would be behind by about 2.5 to 1 and would still be getting the right price to call. Even if you are dominated by A-K or K-Q, you are still getting a decent price to call, as you would need about 3 to 1 on your money. Since you are getting such a good price, and since you wouldn't be risking your whole tournament, calling is an excellent play here, even though it means spending a lot more than you would like to risk with just K♦ 9♣.

You call and he turns over A-J offsuit, which is the sort of hand you were expecting him to hold. You were getting 2.5 to 1 on your money when you only needed 1.7 to 1, so you know you've made the right decision regardless of how the cards come out. A king comes out on the flop, your opponent doesn't improve, and you eliminate a player while continuing to accumulate chips.

The key learning here is that when you get caught stealing blinds with weak or marginal hands, do not muck your hand right away. Think about how much more it will cost you to call, and try to put your opponent on a reasonable range of hands.

Remember that you don't want to miss an opportunity to accumulate chips and win this sit-and-go.

WHEN YOU ARE THE SHORT STACK

Playing a short stack is difficult because opponents who have more chips than you will be looking to call you and knock you out. They will think that you are desperate and willing to move in with weak hands—and they will be right! Nevertheless, you cannot just sit around waiting for pocket aces. You will need to embrace the risk associated with playing live cards by sometimes getting your money in when you are behind. Why? Because you desperately need to double up or at least steal a few blinds.

A rule of thumb that you can use to find out if you are short-stacked is to compare your chip total to the opening pot, which is simply the sum of the blinds and antes. You are short-stacked if your chip stack is less than five opening pots. For example, if the blinds are $150/$300 with $50 antes and there are six players left, the opening pot is $750 ($450 from the blinds plus $300 from the antes). If you have $7,500 in chips you have ten opening pots and you are not short-stacked. If you have fewer than five opening pots, or less than $3,750, you are short-stacked.

When you are a short stack, the only play you have is to move in preflop when you play a hand. When you have a marginal hand, moving in will sometimes make opponents fold and you will win the blinds and antes. It's always a great thing when you steal the blinds and antes, because it allows you to hang around and wait to pick up a strong hand with which to double up. Still, a lot of the time you will get called and you will just have to hope that you win a coin flip or get lucky if your hand is behind. When you have a strong hand, you should also move in because opponents often will assume that your hand is weak; therefore you will have an excellent opportunity to get action and double up.

THE BEST TIMES TO MOVE IN WITH A SHORT STACK

The best spot in which to get all of your money in as a short stack is when there are tight players sitting in the blinds. Tight players are uncomfortable playing big pots with marginal hands so they will often fold, even with favorable pot odds. They might fold decent hands such as A-10, K-Q, K-J or pocket eights shorthanded, even when they are getting better than 2 to 1 on their money. Playing these hands in big pots simply is not part of their strategy. Weak-tight and average-tight players often approach tournaments with a game plan that mostly involves waiting patiently for strong holdings and avoiding playing trouble hands that might be dominated. Many of these players are ineffective in Level A satellites because they fail to make the appropriate adjustments; they continue to play very tight as the blinds increase and the table becomes shorthanded. Look to rebuild your chip stack by frequently raising and stealing the blinds of excessively tight players.

In addition to moving in when tight players are sitting in the blinds, you should also move in when the players sitting in the blinds have medium-sized stacks, or when limpers have medium-sized stacks. A medium stack usually has more than five opening pots but no more than ten. Another way of identifying a medium stack is seeing a chip stack that is slightly below the average chip stack at the table. For example, at a table with six players left, the average chip stack is $2,000, assuming the blinds are at a reasonable level like $100/$200. Therefore, a medium stack would be in the range of $1,600-$2,000. You can calculate the average chip stack like this: Ten players started the sit-and-go with $1,200 chips each, so there are $12,000 chips in play on the table. Divided by the six players left, the average chip stack is $2,000.

The reason to avoid short stacks is that they might feel desperate enough to gamble and call with a wide range of hands. The reason to avoid larger stacks is that they have enough chips to gamble to try to take you out. A commonly employed strategy for someone playing a medium stack is to wait around for a strong hand and to occasionally attempt a blind steal. It follows that the best way for you to capitalize on this strategy is to move in on these opponents when you have a short stack, thus challenging them to risk most of their chips with a marginal hand.

Another decent spot in which to steal the blinds is when no one has raised or limped in front of you, since there is a smaller chance that you will run into a strong hand. However, since your opponents might notice that this is a good spot in which to bluff, you should tighten your range of starting hands somewhat in this situation. You wouldn't want to make this play with 7-4 offsuit only to get called by A-8 or Q-J.

As a side note, when I play online single-table sit-and-goes and multi-table tournaments, I rarely make a play at the blinds without a strong hand in this situation because it seems like I always get called. In live Level A satellites, players will fold a little more often, so I'm more likely to make this play. Still, I don't like to get carried away with it by pushing with a weak hand every time players fold around to me.

Here is a summary of those situations when you should be willing to move in as a short stack. Memorize this short list because it will come in handy at the tables. You should be more willing to move in when there are:

1. Tight players in the blinds
2. Medium-stacked opponents
3. No limpers in front of you

Avoid going all-in with a weak hand after an opponent raises in front of you since there is a very good chance that you will get called. It is more likely that an opponent raises because he likes his hand than it is because he is stealing the blinds, so you need to be careful. Also, when there are multiple limpers in front of you, the risk of getting called increases quite a bit. The limps mean that your opponents have some level of interest in seeing a flop, so avoid shoving in this situation. All it takes to thwart your plan is for one opponent to make a loose call with K-10 suited or with pocket fives and win, so it is best to wait around for a better spot in which to make your move. Remember that when you move in with a marginal hand, it is preferable that your opponents fold so that you can stick around long enough to get paid off with a stronger hand.

MOVE-IN HANDS WITH A SHORT STACK

Here is a list of the starting hands you are looking to move in with as a short stack:

1. **Any ace.** You want everyone to fold if you don't have a strong ace, or to get called by a player with K-Q, K-J, K-10, Q-J or Q-10. You also wouldn't be in bad shape if someone called you with a small pocket pair. Moving in with any ace becomes a better play as the table becomes short-handed since you would stand less risk of getting called by a bigger ace.

2. **K-Q, K-J, K-10.** You want everyone to fold or to get called by a player with a weaker king. You also wouldn't be in bad shape if someone called with ace-high and a weak kicker or a low pocket pair. Once again, as the table gets shorthanded, these hands become a little stronger.

3. **Q-J, Q-10, Q-9.** These are marginal hands no matter how shorthanded the table is, but you could still have live cards if you get called. You wouldn't be in bad shape if someone calls with ace-high and a weak kicker, king-high and a weak kicker, or a low pocket pair.

4. **Any pair.** You are hoping everyone folds if you have a pair of sevens or lower because if you get called, you could be dominated by a higher pocket pair. Otherwise, you want to get called by someone playing a lower pair. Also, you wouldn't be in bad shape against two overcards.

5. **Low suited connectors and one-gappers** such as 9-8 suited, 8-6 suited, 7-5 suited. These are speculative hands and you would certainly need to get lucky to win with them. However, the advantage

of playing these hands is that, unless you get called by an overpair, you will probably have live cards instead of running into a dominating hand such as K-J vs. A-K or A-6 vs. A-Q.

I prefer moving in with a hand like Q-9 rather than a very low pocket pair such as 3-3. Quite often, an opponent with a pair as low as fives will call you, and he will have you dominated by about 4.5 to 1. With Q-9, it would be more coincidental and just poor luck if an opponent had a hand such as A-Q, A-9 or K-Q, not to mention Q-Q or 9-9. You would not be as badly dominated by some of these hands as you would with a low pocket pair against a higher pair. Also, many opponents would fold some of the hands that dominate Q-9; for example, K-9, Q-J and Q-10. If you push with queen-high, most likely you would be behind by about 1.7 to 1 or 1.4 to 1, which are not terrible odds against hands such as A-J, A-10, and A-8 down to A-2, K-J and K-10. You might also get called by a low pair, in which case you would merely need to win a coin flip to double up.

The reason I like to push with suited connectors like 9-8, 7-6 or 6-5 is that these hands aren't dominated by some of the strongest starting hands like A-K, A-Q, A-J, K-Q and K-J. Also, if I get called and I happen to be up against an overpair, my hand will usually be behind by less than 4 to 1, and sometimes quite a bit less. For example, 6♦ 5♦ vs. J♥ J♠ is behind by about 3.3 to 1. By comparison, with a dominated pocket pair, my hand will be behind by about 4.5 to 1.

DON'T MAKE A SMALL RAISE WITH A SMALL STACK

Unless you are holding pocket aces, kings or queens, never make a small raise preflop when you are short-stacked. Raising a small amount isn't an effective play because it usually entices an opponent to play a flop with you. Playing a flop is problematic because it opens up the possibilities that your opponent bets you off the winning hand or outflops you with a hand he would have folded if you had moved in. Let's say the blinds are $150/$300 with a $50 ante. There are four players left and you have $2,300 in chips, so you only have three opening pots left. You are under the gun holding J-J and you start to contemplate making a minimum raise to $600. Your initial thinking is that pocket jacks might be the best starting hand you will see for the rest of the sit-and-go, so you want to ensure that you get action. However, you should instead realize the folly of this idea.

Here is what you need to think about in this situation. According to the table in Appendix B, there is only a 43 percent chance that there will be no overcards on the flop. This means there is a pretty good chance you will be playing a difficult flop. If your minimum raise gets called and the flop comes with two overcards, you will probably have to fold if your opponent bets. If the flop comes with one overcard you will probably have to call because your opponent might have only second pair, a small pocket pair, or maybe a draw, and you can't risk folding the best hand in that situation. However, you would be guessing, and if you are beaten, you might only have two outs, which is a terrible position to be in.

Another fact to consider is that you will have spent more than 25 percent of your chip stack just to put yourself in this difficult position. Hopefully you can see that the minimum raise isn't an effective weapon when you are short-stacked. Keep in mind that when you have a lot of chips, you can embrace the complexity of postflop play in no-limit hold'em tournaments, but when you are short-stacked you should remove this complexity by moving in preflop.

MANAGE YOUR CHIPS ON THE BATTLEFIELD

The most effective way to play a short stack is to manage your remaining chips just as an army general manages his troops on a battlefield. A general avoids dividing his forces if they are relatively small, because if his first small group of troops fails, his remaining troops will likely fail as well, and for similar reasons. Therefore, the general might as well apply maximum pressure on his enemy by sending in all his troops at once.

The same reasoning applies to tournament poker. If your first small bet fails to win you the pot when you are short stacked, your remaining chips will likely fail as well. Some players think making a small raise is an effective way to bluff since it signals that you are seeking action with a monster hand. However, you will still be a long shot to win the blinds that way. Only a very tight and inexperienced player might fold his big blind to a small raise from a short stack. Moreover, if your raise gets called preflop, you will be forced to continue representing a big starting hand by moving in regardless of what comes out on the flop. Since your all-in bet will be small compared to what is already in the pot, your opponent will likely call if he hits any piece of the flop or, sometimes, if he has just a small pocket pair.

In short, don't get too fancy when you are short-stacked. Either move in or fold.

KEY TAKEAWAY

Manage your short stack like an army general manages his troops on a battlefield. Avoid dividing your forces by making small bets—either move in or fold.

MISPLAYING A HAND

Here is an example of how you can misplay a hand by failing to go all-in preflop. Let's say the blinds are $100/$200 with six players left and you have $1,400 in chips. You have less than five opening pots. You are on the button holding Q♠ 10♠, and there is one limper in front of you. You raise to $500 hoping everyone folds or at least hoping for a good flop if someone calls. However, after taking a long time to think and after seeming somewhat unsure of himself, an average-tight player in the big blind goes all-in. He started the hand with $1,600, so he has you covered. The limper folds and the action is back on you. There is $2,400 in the pot and you have $900 left in chips, so you are getting about 2.7 to 1 on your money to call.

You don't have a strong hand, but even though your Q-10 suited could be dominated by A-Q, A-10, K-Q or K-10, this is a mandatory call. Based on your read of your opponent, and the fact that you have a queen and a 10 in your hand, it is highly unlikely that he has pocket queens, pocket tens or A-Q. It is also unlikely that he pushed with K-10.

While you might be up against one of a few dangerous hands, you don't think he is holding a very strong hand, and there are even more hands your opponent could be holding that would easily give you the right price to call. If he has A-J, you only need about 1.4 to 1 on your money. If he has an ace with a 9-kicker or lower, you would only need about 1.1 to 1. Even if he has A-K offsuit, you would only need about 1.5 to 1. Finally, if he has any pocket pair lower than 10-10, you would only need even money.

After evaluating the pot odds and realizing that your chip total could drop to $600 if you fold and the blinds come around again without picking up a playable hand, you call. Your opponent turns over A♥ 3♣. His hand holds up and you are eliminated.

Here is the problem with how you played your hand. Had you simply moved in with your Q♠ 10♠ instead of raising to $500, your opponent would have had a more difficult call and he probably would have folded. He didn't hesitate because he thought your small raise signaled a monster hand—he hesitated because he sensed weakness in your play and he needed to draw up the courage to put his tournament life on the line by playing back at the raiser with a weak ace. Since he was getting short-stacked, he was probably planning to take control of the hand by moving in with his A-3 offsuit if nobody raised. Unfortunately, your play on the button didn't convince him to revise that plan. By failing to apply the appropriate pressure on the big blind, you gave him an opportunity to play back at you. Consequently, you found yourself in a situation where you were the one who had to commit the rest of his chips.

When you are the short stack, be the one to put your opponents to a decision in a big pot, and avoid being the one who is forced to make the call.

In summary, just as you would gamble and call short stacks when you have a lot of chips, so other players with chips will gamble and try to take you out. You need to embrace risk when you are a short stack instead of waiting to pick up a big hand and risk getting blinded out. Also, when you have a playable hand, do not make a conventional raise. Move in preflop most of the time. Of course, you always hope that your hand isn't dominated. But if it is and you get knocked out, just go sign up for another Level A sit-and-go. Sometimes things won't go your way. However, when they do go your way and you start to accumulate chips, you will stand a better chance to win the Level A sit-and-go than anyone else at the table.

A QUICK 'N DIRTY WAY TO MAKE DEALS IN LEVEL A

I don't play Level A satellites with the objective of selling my Level B vouchers. Since Level B satellites are where I make really good money, I do everything I can to collect those vouchers. This includes making deals heads-up in Level A to end the match and guarantee that I collect my prize. If you have a chip lead heads-up in level A, be willing to offer your opponent some cash out of your pocket for him to concede first place to you so that you can get that Level B voucher.

In the chapter called The Science of the Deal, you will learn exactly how much you should be willing to offer opponents when you want to make a deal. The chapter is aptly named because it teaches you a simple mathematical model that ensures you don't give too much away when you have a chip lead, or squander opportunities to make money even when you are behind in the chip count. Feel free to read ahead and consult the model in that chapter in order to learn how much you should offer an opponent in level A. However, since the amount of money in the prize pool in Level A is about one-ninth of that in Level B, you may not need to be so scientific. You may prefer to just rely on your instincts and think of an amount that seems fair to you when you are playing heads-up in level A.

Nevertheless, here is a quick and dirty approach to deal making when you are heads-up in Level A. You should only be willing to negotiate if you have a chip lead. If you are behind in chips, you aren't interested in conceding first place just so that you can sign up for another Level A sit-and-go with a couple hundred extra bucks in your pocket. Given how much more money will be at stake when you are in this same position in level B, you should do everything you can to win that Level B voucher. This includes playing out the heads-up match even if you are behind in chips by as much as 4 to 1. There is simply too much value in playing out the match. After all, with just one double up you would be right back in it.

WHEN YOU ARE THE CHIP LEADER

Here is what to do when you have the chip lead. If you have a 3 to 1 chip lead or better, you shouldn't offer your opponent a deal. He would have to catch a pretty lucky run of cards to stage a comeback and win, so try to get maximum value for your Level A buy-in by winning the Level B voucher without coughing up any extra cash.

However, if you have less than a 3 to 1 chip lead, you can offer your opponent $100 or $200 in cash, in addition to his free replay, to concede first place to you. Be willing to make this deal because you don't want to give your opponent a chance to catch up and win, which he can easily do since you don't have a dominant chip lead. If $100 or $200 cash isn't enough to persuade your opponent to concede, you could increase your offer to $300 or even $400.

Now, let's assume that you've won your Level A satellite, or you've made a deal at the end. You're ready to move up to a Level B satellite, where you can really make some money. The next section teaches you how to maximize your profit potential in Level B events while minimizing your risks.

8 HOW TO PLAY LEVEL B SATELLITES

In Level B you need to take on just a little more risk than in an online single-table sit-and-go because finishing in the top two doesn't happen just by showing up. You will still need to work for your chips.

Compared to Level A sit-and-goes, Level B satellites require more patience because they are more about survival than they are about rapidly trying to accumulate chips. Whereas highly aggressive poker is your mantra in Level A and extreme patience is a rewarding virtue in online sit-and-goes, occasional aggression is the best approach in level B.

YOUR LEVEL B OBJECTIVE: REACH HEADS-UP PLAY

You will still want to play somewhat carefully in Level B because your only goal is to make it to a heads-up match, with or without a big chip lead. You don't need to actually win to make big money. Once you have assured yourself of a top-two finish, you will be in a position to decide whether you are willing to work out a deal or whether you prefer to play it out to win a Main Event seat. That decision will depend on the relative size of your chip stack, the skill level of your opponent, and your personal financial objectives.

Making it to the top two gives you a chance to negotiate a deal with $10,300 in the prize pool (though this amount could be more or less depending on the big-money tournament you choose). That's enough money to motivate almost any opponent to work out a deal!

If you already have a Main Event seat, your objective might be to negotiate for cash. Or if you really feel like competing, if you have a big chip lead, or if you think that your opponent is a weaker player, you could decide to forego a deal and try to win another seat, which you can sell later on. And even if you haven't already won a seat, you could decide that a guaranteed cash profit is important to you and is not worth risking by playing it out to win. The point here is that once you are heads-up, you have a number of options at your disposal.

KEY TAKEAWAY

Your objective is to make it to the final two in level B. Then you can decide to either work out a deal for cash or try to win a seat.

STRATEGIC OVERVIEW

Play the first blind level and the late stages of a Level B satellite conservatively, just like you would play an online single-table sit-and-go. It's important to play slowly in the very early stages of Level B to ensure that you don't risk losing a lot of chips or get knocked out before your weaker opponents. As you get a little deeper into a Level B satellite, you can start to take advantage of your tight image by raising preflop more often and by trying to outplay your opponents after the flop, especially when you have position. However, as you will learn in the next section, you will still need to play small-pot poker to conserve enough chips to survive to second place.

As you get a little more active in the middle stages, you will need to think about your table image and how to make plays at the right times. What you really want is to control the table without allowing your opponents to realize what you're doing. You will not want them to think you're a loose cannon because you'll start to get callers every time you bet or raise. Getting callers can be a problem because you won't have a strong hand often enough to justify the action.

HOW TO CONTROL THE TABLE

The best way for you to control the table is with great timing. Unfortunately, playing a tight, conservative game can sometimes lull you to sleep. Take advantage of your tight image after the early stages by becoming more active in the right spots. Here are some of the things you will need to do. Keep in mind that you will want to space out these plays so that your opponents don't think you are a loose player.

MAKE CONTINUATION BETS

Following up on a preflop raise by betting out after the flop is the right play most of the time. You don't often want to just give up and give your chips away. You want to apply pressure on your opponents when you are in a good position. However, you will still need to vary the frequency of your continuation bets by checking, folding or check-folding sometimes. Doing so will persuade your opponents that you have a hand when you bet.

As a general guide, you should make a continuation bet on almost any type of board about 75 percent of the time when you are heads-up and about 50 percent of the time when you are playing a three-way pot. You don't usually want to bet out on the flop when you get three or more callers preflop.

Even heads-up, the only play to avoid is making a continuation bet against a good player on a low board like 8♦ 4♥ 3♣. A good player will know that you are trying to represent an overpair and he will likely challenge you and give you action.

TAKE A STAB AT POTS

After the flop, when you have position against tight players in an uncontested pot, you should usually fire at the pot to try to win it right there. You will often have these types of opportunities to pick up pots, so you must remain aware at the table so that you don't let these chances slip away. Even when you miss the flop completely, be sure to follow the action because if tight opponents check, you will have a chance to win some chips.

USE THE STOP-AND GO PLAY
AGAINST BLIND STEALERS

This means calling a raise preflop and betting into the raiser on the flop, even if you have nothing. This play is more effective than reraising preflop because it prevents your opponent from shutting you out by moving in with solid hands like A-K, A-Q, A-J, K-Q, or a pocket pair. There is only a 32 percent chance that your opponent will pair one of his hole cards on the flop. Further, there is a strong likelihood of at least one overcard appearing on the flop if your opponent has a pocket pair other than aces or kings. Therefore, the higher percentage play is for you to make a move on the flop because your opponent will have a tough time sticking around if he missed it badly.

By using the stop-and-go play you will accomplish two things. First, you will accumulate chips. If an opponent routinely raises your blinds, you will be able to win some chips back by spacing out these plays and persuading your opponent that you have a hand. Second, you will prevent opponents from raising your blinds every chance they get. While you should always avoid getting into emotionally charged wars, you will need to let blind stealers know that you won't fold every time they raise. By occasionally taking a stand, you will convince your opponents to make less steal attempts.

The stop-and-go play is effective against weaker opponents, but against stronger players it is less effective because they know that the more common play when you outflop a preflop raiser is to check and let him bet into you. Therefore, betting into the raiser often signals that you don't have a strong hand. Against good players, a check-raise will be more effective because it will let them know that if they keep playing with you, they will have to play a big pot.

KEEP THE POT SMALL

Remember to keep the pots relatively small when you bluff so that you don't often risk losing a lot of chips without a strong hand. If you make a steal-bet after the flop, back off if someone is on to you and plays back at you. Do not allow yourself to get fooled into playing a big pot with a marginal hand just because you think your opponent might be playing back at you with nothing. Even if an opponent bluffs you off a pot and shows you the bluff, respond by slowing down and waiting to trap him with a strong hand. Do not get frustrated because that will cause you to make plays you will regret.

You can even take advantage of those moments when you have to back off following a failed bluff attempt. After you start to loosen up a little in the middle stages, losing some small pots can make you look like a weak player, which can set you up for a big payoff later on. While you will certainly try to accumulate chips with some moves, do not panic if a few of them fail because in Level B, you have plenty of time to shift into a lower gear and wait for strong hands. Varying your play in this way will help in disguising your master plan to merely survive until second place. By changing gears, you can confuse your opponents, and some of them will eventually fall into your trap when you are holding a big hand.

WHEN YOU'RE GETTING CLOSE

As you approach the final stages of level B, avoid taking on a lot of risk, just like in the end game of an online single-table sit-and-go. Since you will be so close to reaching your goal, you will need to make sure you don't squander your opportunity by overreacting to the rising blind levels and playing too loose. Be prepared to fold a lot of hands and to let your opponents play at each other. Hopefully they will knock each other out, which will bring you closer to a second place finish. You should even be willing to squeak into second place with a very small chip stack if you have to because you can still work out a deal heads-up with an opponent who has a big chip lead.

The only time you will need to play fast in the end game is if you are on a short stack and four or five players are still left. In that case, you won't have an opportunity to wait around for strong hands so you will need to force the issue by putting yourself in a position to accumulate chips. You will need to loosen up and start betting all your chips with hands that give you a decent chance to double up and get back into the game in case you get called. The range of hands you should use as a short stack in Level B is the same range you were taught to use as a short stack in level A, so please consult that chapter for the list of starting hands.

SMALL-POT POKER

Since you need to accumulate some chips to ensure that you can go deep into the sit-and-go without being forced to play a short stack, small-pot poker is a very effective style throughout most stages of level B. Identify weak-tight and average-tight players early on so you can try to play pots with them. Take advantage of what I call The Minefield Effect by moving these opponents off their hands on fourth and fifth streets, and try to steal their blinds.

> ### THE MINEFIELD EFFECT:
>
> Just as a person who walks deep into a minefield fears that a mine is due to explode, so a tight poker player fears playing a hand all the way to the river.

With lengthy blind levels and deeper starting stacks ($3,000 in chips), you will have many opportunities to outplay opponents while having enough chips to avoid putting yourself in danger of becoming severely short stacked in case some of these plays don't work. Since you will have ample time to outplay opponents, you will also need to change gears and slow down quite often in order to keep opponents guessing about the strength of your hand and to ensure that you don't gradually bluff all your chips away.

HOW TO KEEP YOUR OPPONENTS OFF BALANCE

By mixing things up and playing moderately aggressive poker, your opponents will never know where they are in a hand with you—that's exactly what you want. Creating doubt and confusion in your opponents' minds will either cause them to avoid playing hands with you, which makes it easier to steal their blinds, or will cause them to make a mistake against you when you are holding a strong hand.

USE THE STOP-AND-GO PLAY

You don't have to be in the blinds to use this play. You can call a preflop raise from any position and then represent a hand after the flop. I recommend making this play following an opponent's preflop raise when he is in position, because there is a higher likelihood that he is holding a weak starting hand.

If you are going to bet the flop in a multiway pot, a ragged rainbow board such as Q♦ 7♣ 3♥ is best because it won't be likely to interest your opponents.

APPLY PRESSURE FROM THE CUTOFF
AND BUTTON AFTER THE FLOP

By playing position when you are bluffing, you increase the odds of coming out ahead. Forcing opponents to play out of position makes it tougher for them to keep playing with you all the way to the river.

One example of this is to wait for a scare card against a tight opponent. Let's say the blinds are $50/$100 and you have $2,800 in chips. A tight opponent raises in middle position to $300. He has about $2,000 in chips. You call in the cutoff position with 9♦ 6♦. The flop is J♥ 7♣ 5♣. All you've got is a gutshot straight draw. Your opponent bets $400, a seemingly standard continuation bet and you call hoping to take the pot away from him on the turn or river. You are putting him on A-K, A-Q, K-Q or maybe pocket nines or tens. However, if he keeps betting, you might have to put him on A-J or even an overpair and back off this hand. If an ace or a king had come on this flop, you might think twice about making this play, but you can't be certain that your opponent has hit anything on this board.

The turn is the 4♥, so the board is showing J♥ 7♣ 5♣ 4♥. You still have just a gutshot draw. Your opponent checks, signaling that he might be willing to give up. You bet $500, he folds and shows pocket tens. The overcard certainly scared him, but when the turn card brought a possible straight, he decided he was beaten. By betting the turn, you also were representing a pair of jacks and you wanted to prevent your opponent from drawing out on you on the river.

REPRESENT POCKET ACES WITH AN EARLY POSITION RAISE

This play is used quite often online these days, but it is still very effective and it can be a quick way to win a few chips. Simply raise preflop with any two hole cards, and then fire on the flop and turn almost regardless of what comes off, as though you had pocket aces. This is a risky play that requires deviating from your small pot poker game plan for one hand. Therefore, you will want to make sure that you haven't been active for a while in order to persuade opponents that you have what you are representing. Be sure to back off any action on the river if you continue to get action on the turn, unless you think there is a good chance that an opponent missed a draw and you don't think your hand would win a showdown.

MAKE AN UNUSUAL BET SUCH AS A MINIMUM RAISE

A minimum preflop raise, especially from early or middle position, can confuse your opponents. Some opponents will think you are seeking action with pocket aces or kings, while others will think you are making a weak bet with a hand such as J-10 suited and you just want to see a flop. Creating confusion with a minimum bet can often work in your favor: You can represent a big drawing hand on a flop like 9♦ 7♠ 4♠, or you can represent A-K or A-Q on an ace-high or king-high flop. Also, a minimum preflop raise helps keep the pot small, so you won't lose a lot of chips if someone reraises you preflop or bets into you after the flop and you have to fold.

In the middle and late stages of level B, the minimum raise can become more than just a novelty play. When you are holding a playable hand like A-10 five-handed when the blinds and antes are high, it is likely to be the best starting hand. Therefore, you should raise the pot. The advantage of making a minimum raise is that it ensures that you don't ruin your tournament by playing a very big pot if you miss the flop.

Also, when the blinds and antes are high, even a minimum raise will quite often win you the blinds. Opponents will think that you are seeking action with a strong hand and that they must hold a strong starting hand to risk getting involved in what could develop into a big pot. Therefore, they will often be willing to give up their blinds.

RERAISE BEFORE THE FLOP

Although this isn't a play that is normally part of a small pot poker player's repertoire, you can occasionally put in a reraise bluff preflop to push an opponent off a hand such as A-10, K-Q, K-J or J-10 suited. This play is most effective five- or six-handed against tighter opponents with medium sized chip stacks. When the table starts to get shorthanded, some tight opponents will loosen their starting hand requirements a little. You can take advantage of this by challenging them to play a big pot with a marginal hand. By reraising, you are signaling that you have a big hand and if they want to risk most or all of their chips by playing with you, they had better have a big hand.

KEEP THE POT SMALL

You might think that the skill level of your opponents will make it more difficult for you to play small-pot poker in level B, which is a strategy that involves outplaying your opponents after the flop. You might think that if people can afford to pay the $1,240 out of their pockets or have won their Level B vouchers, they are experienced players. The reality is there are always enough weak players to prey on in Level B in order to build your chip stack. Some players can afford to buy into the $1,240 satellite because they simply have the money, which doesn't necessarily come from a poker bankroll, while others just got lucky when they won their voucher in the Level A sit-and-go. Sometimes you will be blessed with an entire table full of weak-tight players and you can build up a large chip stack quickly. Weak-tight opponents will probably avoid playing pots with you and might stop raising you or stop calling your raises, which will make it much easier for you to finish in the top two.

Small-pot poker is the best approach in Level B because it allows you to accumulate chips without risking a lot in any one hand so that you can survive until the top two. This approach encourages you to stay active, which makes your play unpredictable—and it is unpredictability that causes people to make mistakes against you.

If you take some time to observe other Level B satellites in action, you will notice aggressive players getting all their money in preflop with pocket kings or queens and getting paid off by opponents holding hands like A-10 or low pocket pairs such as sixes or fives. It is also common to see aggressive players win big pots after the flop with just top pair/good kicker against someone holding top pair with a weaker kicker or sometimes just second pair. When you see this happening, it means that players are making mistakes by choosing the wrong times to fight back. That is why small-pot poker is an effective strategy. Playing a lot of hands, gambling cheaply to see if you hit a big flop, and betting frequently after the flop will lead you to success in the key middle stages of level B. Weaker players will find it difficult to stop the momentum that you build by using this style of play.

CHANGING GEARS

While you need to be aggressive to accumulate chips, realize that the type of small pot poker you want to play is more conservative than in a Level A sit-and-go. Remember that the aforementioned moves in your small pot repertoire need to be spaced out or else you will fail to get your opponents to fold and you will lose most of your chips. Remember the rule that you never want to get knocked out of a Level B sit-and-go before the weaker players are eliminated. Therefore, while you will play a little more aggressively than most players at the table, you will still need to change gears frequently. After all, this is not an online turbo satellite with only three-minute blind levels. Your chips are valuable and you don't want to waste them, so you need to play intelligently.

With thirty-minute blinds and deeper starting stacks, you will face some opponents who like to wait patiently for a monster hand, hoping to get paid off by a loose player. If you are holding a hand like top pair with a medium kicker, and you are getting action from a tight player who seems experienced, you may need to use your radar to determine whether you are beaten, and you may need to consider folding a solid made hand. You will want to be especially wary of getting all your chips in and risking your whole tournament without having a very strong hand against a tight, experienced player. Remember that there is a lot of value in finishing in the top two, so don't do anything that will jeopardize your chances.

Play aggressive poker against the right players in order to accumulate chips, but take on the appropriate amount of risk so that you can survive long enough to make money. In almost every Level B satellite you play, you will have to fold a good hand at least once, so be prepared to implement this survival technique.

Stay away from other aggressive players if you can because these players are less predictable and harder to control. Try to take pots down when they don't take the lead with a raise preflop, and in general look to play pots with weaker players. You don't need to beat a quality opponent—you just need to have enough chips to be able to make a deal with him or her in the end. You don't want to be the first or second player eliminated just because you wanted to outplay another aggressive player. Always avoid a head-to-head war that will distract you from your ultimate objective of playing heads up. When there are still weak players with lots of chips to give away, you must stick around long enough to take their chips.

> **KEY TAKEAWAY**
>
> Target weaker players to play pots against. Avoid very good and very aggressive opponents.

WHEN TO SHIFT GEARS

To help you judge when to change gears by adjusting the number of hands you play and the number of risky moves you make, think about where you stand relative to the average chip stack at the table. To calculate the average chip stack, take the total number of chips in play and divide it by the number of players left. Here is an example. If the sit-and-go began with ten people and $3,000 starting chips, the number of chips in play is $30,000. To get the average stack, divide $30,000 by the number of players left. If you have $10,000 in chips with four players left, you have $2,500 more chips than the average chip stack of $7,500, which means that you are on track to finish in the top two.

If you are above the average chip stack, you are doing well so you might choose to slow down for a little while. You already have the chip stack that your opponents wish they had, so you shouldn't waste it by playing like a canon. If you start to raise preflop every second hand or try to outplay opponents every time you see a flop, you could very quickly give away most of your chips.

Here is an even simpler way of gaining perspective on where you stand in a sit-and-go. Let's say you have one quarter of the chips in play with six people left. An average stack is one sixth of the chips in play, so you are clearly ahead of the curve and in position to finish in the top two. The same can be said if you have one third of the chips in play with four people left, where the average stack is one quarter of the chips in play. At that point, you won't need to continue taking on a lot of risk, so you should look to slow down and find opportunities to get your money in when you are ahead in small to medium sized pots.

When you are ahead of the curve and in a good position to finish in the top two, avoid playing pots against opponents who also have a lot of chips. Since you don't need to win big pots from these opponents in order to finish in the top two, don't risk making a mistake against them or giving them a chance to get lucky and take most of your chips. Instead focus your attention on players with smaller chip stacks but do so responsibly; try to get your money in when you are ahead against the short stacks.

Notice that this is a different approach to playing against short stacks than what I recommend in level A. Since you need to chase chips to win a Level A sit-and-go, it stands to reason that you should risk a portion of your large stack when your hand is behind, assuming you are getting a good price to call. In level B, never make the mistake of thinking that owning a large stack gives you a license to recklessly bully opponents or to call off your stack in big pots in order to knock out an opponent. Second place is still very desirable, so you will not want to waste the chips you have earned. Always keep thinking about where you are relative to your opponents' chip stacks and manage your risk accordingly.

THE FIRST BLIND LEVEL

While you still need to accumulate some chips to avoid playing a short stack for most of this sit-and-go, the decisions you make in the first blind level will be far more conservative compared to those you would make in the first blind level of a Level A satellite. In Level B you get twice as much time to play each blind level and more than twice as many starting chips, which makes you about half as desperate to accumulate chips during the first blind level.

Do not try to outplay opponents on every flop and do not often raise preflop without a strong hand. Preflop raisers are more likely to be holding big hands in the first blind level so reraising isn't a very good play this early. Also, stealing blinds isn't a great play because the blinds are so small that there isn't anything worth stealing.

You can still take the lead in a few hands, but you can also accomplish a lot by sitting back, observing your opponents, and identifying the weaker players. Occasionally you can gamble cheaply to try to hit a big flop. Instead of making high risk reraises preflop, try to just call raises with solid starting hands or speculative hands in order to outflop someone who doesn't have the sense to fold a hand when he is beaten.

By playing mostly conventional and premium starting hands and by avoiding making high-risk moves, you may develop a tight image at the table in the first blind level. Since opponents might think you are tight, you will be able to control the pots you play at $50/$100 and beyond in order to make opponents fold without holding strong cards. After the first blind level, those pots will also be larger and more meaningful. By the time your opponents catch on to the fact that you are not really a tight player, you might already have a large chip stack.

At $25/$50 you are mostly looking to win chips off players who overvalue top pair with a weak kicker, especially when they pair an ace, so playing strong conventional hands like A-K, A-Q, and A-J can be effective. You will also play small pairs and suited connectors and look to hit a big flop or at least a big drawing hand. You rarely want to be all-in preflop at $25/$50 unless you are holding pocket aces, kings or queens. However, feel free to come over the top for a third raise with A-K preflop because many opponents will fold a middle pair as high as 10-10. Even with pocket queens or jacks, some opponents might just call a third raise to make sure an overcard doesn't hit the flop. However, do not go all-in with A-K—finishing in the top two is too valuable for you to risk your whole sit-and-go in a possible coin flip situation this early.

Big drawing hands with twelve outs or more are also worth playing aggressively because there is no guarantee that you will hold a hand with as much potential to win a big pot. However, avoid going all-in during the first blind level on a draw because you will get called more often than you think, and usually by someone holding top pair with the best kicker or with an overpair. Getting called in that situation means you will be in a coin flip and that is not what you want this early in the tournament. Instead, look to apply pressure by making a normal sized raise against an opponent that you think is capable of folding.

AFTER THE FIRST BLIND LEVEL

The second blind level is where you can start building your chip stack. Blinds are $50/$100 so pots are at least big enough to interest you. Also, the blind level after $50/$100 is $100/$200 and at that level any raised pot can become very large, so you will want to have enough chips to do battle without feeling desperately short stacked. After the first blind level you will have a pretty good idea who the weak-tight players are, so you can start raising their blinds more liberally and outplaying them after the flop. However, keep in mind that with 30-minute intervals you will still want to change gears quite a bit. You especially want to avoid falling into a tight player's trap when he is just waiting to catch an aggressive player off guard.

Once you pass the first blind level you can start opening up your range of starting hands. This will enable you to play and win more pots, and to eventually begin confusing your opponents so that they can't easily put you on a hand and play well against you. Your range of hands after $25/$50 is almost identical to that for a Level A sit-and-go. You can play A-K down to A-9 because the tighter players who still have a lot of chips will continue to fold hands like A-10 or any other ace with a low kicker.

Keep in mind that some players on a short stack will call or possibly move in with weak aces. That is why I recommend playing aces with a kicker no lower than a 9. You must have the best of it in an all-in situation this early in the tournament, and you don't want to end up playing a big pot with A-3 against a short stack's A-8. You can also start raising with any suited ace, even A-2 suited, because you are willing to play big pots with big drawing hands like on a flop of 10♣ 5♣ 4♥ when you have A♣ 2♣. You can also play A-5, A-4, A-3, or A-2 offsuit in a raised pot hoping to hit two pair or a wheel with these hands. If you are up against someone with a big ace, you might win a big pot.

Other hands you can play after the first blind level are K-Q, K-J, Q-J, Q-10, any pocket pair, and any suited connector or one-gapper. Sometimes you can raise with low suited connectors if there are tight players in the blinds. Feel free to raise or even reraise preflop with any pocket pair, but you could also just limp in or call one raise hoping to flop a set. If you raise with a hand such as 6-6 and you get one caller, he might have two overcards and only about a 32 percent chance of hitting the flop; therefore, it is usually worthwhile to fire another bet on the flop to make him fold in case you miss your set. If you reraise preflop with a low pair and the initial raiser just called your reraise, you would play it the same way after the flop, since your opponent might have two big cards that he wants to see a flop with first before committing more chips. If the flop comes low and ragged, such as 10-high or worse, you would need to make a solid bet on the flop to capitalize in case your opponent missed it.

Some opponents will be suspicious of a continuation bet, so they might just call and hang around a little longer with a hand like A-K or A-Q, even on a low flop. They might hope that you lose heart on the turn and they can check it down and win with ace-high, or they might even fire a bet if you show weakness by checking. You will have to feel it out when you are in the moment. If you think that your opponent is someone who likes to play conventional cards and you believe he is holding two overcards, you can fire another bet on the turn, but only bet about half the pot, as you don't want to waste too many chips on a bluff. Only if you feel very strongly about your read should you consider moving in. The reason you want to be wary of moving in is that if you are wrong and your opponent has an overpair such as 10-10 or 9-9, he will almost certainly call even though you are representing pocket aces or kings. Most players don't fold overpairs in a single-table sit-and-go. Another reason to fire again on the turn when you are representing a strong hand is that some opponents will hang around and call a bet on the flop with a low pocket pair. They will hope that you check the turn signaling that their pair is good, so a bet on the turn could convince them that their hand is beaten.

Although you will play a wide range of hands, this doesn't mean that you need to bluff at every pot. You still need to change gears to conserve chips, to keep opponents guessing about what you are holding, and to manage your image. If opponents see that you play every hand and are constantly bluffing, they will start to call and raise you more often. Despite your willingness to play almost any two cards, you still need to find the right balance between aggression and patience, which is always the key to getting good results in a single-table sit-and-go.

PLAYING THE END GAME WITH A LARGE CHIP COUNT

As a general rule, when you have a good-sized chip stack or even the chip lead in the end game of level B, you must not waste it by playing too loose. Steal some blinds now and then to maintain your chip count, but avoid situations that could cause you to lose a big pot without a strong hand. This is why I recommend that when you raise preflop, the size of your bet should be double the big blind. In other words, make a minimum raise.

Here is an example of a minimum raise. The blinds are $200/$400 with a $75 ante, and four players are left. You are under the gun with Q♥ J♥ and you have $9,800 in chips. Your bet would be $800. One benefit of raising such a small amount is that if you get called and have to fold to an opponent's bet after missing the flop, you won't lose a lot of chips, and you will have a solid $9,000 left. Since your raise to $800 will still be sizeable and difficult for almost everyone except a chip leader to call, you will win the pot preflop a lot of the time.

Another benefit of this play is that if you get called and you want to make a continuation bet on the flop, you won't have to risk a ton of chips because the pot won't be large. Let's use the same example to illustrate this point. If you raise to $800 and only the big blind calls there would be $2,500 in the pot. Let's say that your opponent has about $8,000 left. If you bet about half the pot (or around $1,250), you would apply a lot of pressure on him. In fact, your bet would apply pressure on any opponent with less than $10,000 left. You are signaling that you are prepared to put both your and your opponent's tournament life on the line by playing a big pot. Even if your opponent hits a small piece of the flop such as bottom pair or he has third pair when he is holding a small pocket pair, you would be forcing him to guess that his hand is good. You wouldn't be risking a ton of chips, and you would be giving yourself a chance to win the pot by making your opponent fold. Betting out is the more profitable play in the long run compared to the situation you are putting your opponent in, which is guess-calling an opponent's continuation bet.

RAISING HANDS IN SHORTHANDED PLAY

Here is a list of premium or otherwise solid starting hands with which you should usually make small raises preflop when the game gets shorthanded:

A-K, A-Q, A-J, A-10

With any unpaired hand you only have a 32 percent chance of making a pair on the flop, so you don't want to commit too many chips before looking at the flop. Remember that to finish in the top two, you mustn't get stubborn by overplaying a pretty starting hand that misses the board.

K-Q, K-J

Again, you don't stand a great chance of seeing a flop you like but these hands are worth raising with since they are often the best starting hands shorthanded.

Q-J OR Q-10 SUITED

Sometimes these are the best hands preflop when the game is short-handed. They also offer an opportunity for you to pick up a drawing hand, in addition to possibly making a pair.

ANY POCKET PAIR

If you are holding a monster like pocket aces, kings or queens, you will want action and a minimum raise could elicit a call from hands like A-7, K-10, or speculative hands like J-10 or 8-6 suited. If you have a small pair you will still likely hold the best hand, so it is worthwhile for you to raise and hope to win the pot preflop.

WHEN TO MAKE A MINIMUM RAISE

You should also make minimum raises when you want to steal the blinds. Despite the small raise, it can be difficult for players to call with weak hands even when they are getting favorable pot odds because they cannot afford to waste chips by gambling. Of course, if an opponent reraises when you are trying to steal the blinds, you can get off your hand without losing a lot of chips.

Let's say that you are in a Level B sit-and-go with five players left and the blinds are $200/$400 with a $75 ante. You have $6,900 in chips and a tight opponent in the big blind has $3,500 left. It is only $400 more for him to call but he will probably view this as a significant portion of his stack. He would need to hold a pretty strong hand to reraise and he would be risking precious chips if he wanted to gamble with a marginal hand just to see if he hit a big flop. Most likely, he is waiting to move in with an ace or a pair, which he won't often have. It is surprising how often you will get tight opponents to fold in this situation, even when they should be embracing risk and pushing in an attempt to get lucky and double up. Try to identify who the tight players are in the end game because you should raise their blinds liberally, which will help you maintain a solid chip stack.

Despite your willingness to repeatedly raise the pot when tight players are sitting in the blinds, still remember that your objective is to finish in the top two, so you don't want to get carried away by playing too loose. You might think that you should play aggressively with a wide range of hole cards when you have a big chip stack four or five-handed. However, bullying is not the right approach in level B. You must tighten up a little to try to get your money in with a solid hand because most players on a short stack, aside from very tight players, will quite often move in preflop. This will force you to wait for a decent ace or a pair to call them.

If the end game is a battle of marginal hands and weak aces, you will benefit by showing a little patience, assuming you have enough chips to wait around for a quality hand.

AVOID COIN FLIPS IN BIG POTS

One very important pointer is to avoid coin flip situations in big pots. When you are so close to a top two finish, you must avoid relying completely on luck to achieve a great tournament result. Let's say there are four players left and the blinds are $300/$600 with $100 antes. You have a little more than an average chip stack of $8,500. You come out raising to $1,400 with pocket eights under the gun. An opponent who has you covered reraises all-in. You don't want to just make a quick call here. Although eights might be the best hand four handed, you could be calling off your tournament on a coin flip if he has two overcards, which isn't something you want to do unless you have to. Of course, there is also a chance your hand is dominated by an overpair. This means that if you call you will either be involved in a coin flip or your hand will be dominated. There is only a small chance that you have him dominated with the higher pocket pair. When you look at it this way, it is clear that calling isn't a great option. You would still have enough chips left to compete after just one small raise, so you would fold in this spot.

Here is another example of playing your hand carefully in the end game. You are holding A-6 offsuit on the button five-handed, and the blinds are $150/$300 with $50 antes. You have $6,900 in chips so you are just a bit above the average stack. A short stack moves in under the gun for $2,800. Many players with your chip stack would instantly call in this situation thinking that their larger stack gives them the license to pick off a short stack with any ace in the hole. While that thinking might make sense if your only objective was to win like it is in a Level A sit-and-go, you need to be more vigilant in these situations since finishing second is almost equally desirable for you.

Let's analyze why this is a bad spot to call off a large portion of your chip stack. You are not playing heads-up, you're at a five-handed table. Your A-6 offsuit could easily be dominated by a larger ace, which would put you at about a 3 to 1 disadvantage. You could also be roughly a 2.4 to 1 underdog if your opponent has a pocket pair from 7-7 up to K-K. Even if he has a pocket pair lower than 6-6, you would still be facing a coin toss. Also, even if you are winning against a hand like K-Q or K-J, you are only about a 1.4 to 1 favorite. It would cost you about 40 percent of your stack to make this call, so do you really want to rely on luck with that much of your chip stack and with a $10,000 prize on the line?

The only type of hand your opponent could be holding that you would be in a great spot against is a speculative bluffing hand such as 8-6 or 7-6, which are hands you are dominating. It would be highly coincidental if he were holding those hands. Also, it is highly unlikely that he is holding an ace with a weaker kicker than a 6, which would mean that you have him dominated.

You are currently above the average stack. If you lose this pot, you will drop well below the average while doubling up one of your competitors. Considering that if you call, you will probably not be in a strong position when the cards are turned over and that it is costing you a lot of your chips to call, you would fold in this situation.

THE FIRST MOVER ADVANTAGE

This leads us to another key lesson about the end game. Having first mover advantage is important. Since it usually takes a better hand to call with than to raise, be willing to fold decent hands if your opponent is the first to get his bet off. Sometimes, you will just need to tip your cap, fold and wait for a better spot to risk a lot of your chips. You don't want to call off a large portion of your stack with a weak hand when you are so close to a top-two finish. Instead, you want to be the one to put your opponents to a tough decision, a play that carries extra value because you gain the option of winning the hand if your opponents fold. First mover advantage is an important concept in the end game. Since the blinds are high, even a small raise can make your opponents fold.

> **KEY TAKEAWAY**
>
> First mover advantage means applying pressure on your opponents before they bet into you to try to win the hand by getting them to fold.

AVOID PLAYING LOW CONNECTORS IN THE END GAME

Playing low suited connectors is not recommended in the end game unless your objective is just to steal the blinds. Unless you have a very large chip stack, you simply cannot afford to waste chips on speculative hands. The best way to think about suited connectors is that you would be looking for a flop that merely gives you drawing opportunities, at which point you would have to risk even more chips to push opponents off their hands or to see if you hit your draw. Unless there are tight players in the blinds and you want to steal the pot preflop, avoid playing speculative hands when the blinds and antes are very high.

BE CAREFUL WHEN PLAYING MARGINAL HANDS

Although this will seem like stating the obvious, another important thing to watch out for in the end game is playing a dominated hand. Sometimes in a four or five-handed game you can hold reasonably strong hands like pocket eights or A-10 only to find yourself up against a dominating hand with your tournament on the line. A key sign that you might be beaten is when you have a sizeable chip stack and you are getting action preflop from another big stack or from a medium stack. You must sometimes resist the temptation to assume your opponents are always playing recklessly loose just because it is the end game. After all, some opponents will recognize that they are also close to the money and they won't want to risk a lot of chips without a strong hand.

The best way to play a marginally strong hand like A-10 is to take the lead preflop with a raise and hope to take the pot down with one continuation bet should you get called. However, you have to be very careful when facing a reraise preflop. Folding some of these hands when facing a reraise can be a good play since coming over the top or even calling might commit you to the pot and cost you your entire stack. Even calling a reraise with A-J when you're four or five-handed isn't a great play since you only have a 32 percent chance of hitting the flop. If your opponent has a pair, he has a significant advantage. Of course, his reraise might also let you know that your ace is dominated by A-K or A-Q. With a low pocket pair such as 6-6, calling a reraise isn't a great play because you are likely to see overcards on the flop. This will make your hand tough to play after the flop, and it might cost you the rest of your chips to find out if you are ahead. When your opponents are putting pressure on you, it is best to fold these types of hands.

Here is an example of how to play a marginally strong hand in the end game. Let's say there are four players left, the blinds are $300/$600 with $100 antes, and you have $9,700 in chips. You get dealt 9-9 under the gun and you raise to $1,200. You are hoping to take the pot down preflop, but if you get one caller, you plan to throw out a continuation bet even if there are overcards on board in an effort to represent top pair. Suddenly the big blind, a weak-tight player, reraises all-in for another $5,500 on top.

While you could have your opponent dominated if he is holding a lower pair, he could also have you crushed with a higher pair. Also, you don't want to risk going up against two overcards in a pot that big because it would be a coin toss. So, even though your weaker opponent might be making the wrong play by pushing with a marginal hand like A-10, you would fold and wait for a better spot to win a big pot. You are not desperate for chips so don't waste the favorable position you are in by gambling with more than half of your chips. Also remember why you made a minimum raise in the first place, which was to be able to get away from your hand if you had to without losing a lot of chips.

What if your opponent didn't move in and he only reraised another $2,000 in this situation? You would have to make a tough decision. There would be $5,700 in the pot so you would be getting about 2.9 to 1 on your money, which seems like a pretty good deal. The problem is that another $2,000 is still a reasonably significant portion of your chip stack (you have $7,500 left) and you might be up against a bigger pair. After all, he just bet more than half his stack and is therefore committed to the pot, so it feels like he is trying to get you all-in. If he has a big ace he might have just pushed in order to avoid playing a flop. Even if you call and there are overcards on the flop, you would still have to risk more chips to find out if he missed. Your bet in this situation would commit you to the pot, meaning that you would have to risk all your chips to play the hand out. Calling and hoping your opponent misses the flop when there is a strong chance you will see overcards or that he has a big pocket pair isn't a high percentage play. Considering that you are already in a pretty good position to finish in the top two, you don't need to take on this risk so folding is a good play. Remember that you made a minimum raise to be able to get away from your hand if you have to without losing a lot of chips.

WHEN AN AGGRESSIVE PLAYER CALLS YOUR RAISE

What would you do if an aggressive opponent with $10,000 chips called your raise on the button and the flop came K♦ 8♠ 4♦? This is a troublesome spot. Your 9-9 in the hole gives you second pair, so there is a good chance that your hand is winning. However, there is an overcard on the flop, which makes it risky for you to play out this hand. Also, it's usually hard to wrestle a pot away from this type of opponent, so even if you are holding the best hand, you might get outplayed since you are out of position. So you start to think through the hands he could be holding.

If your opponent has A-K, wouldn't he have reraised preflop? Perhaps he would have reraised with K-Q. Also, if he has a pocket pair such as J-J or 10-10, he probably would have reraised preflop. This means that if he has a pocket pair, it is probably a hand such as 5-5, and you would have him crushed. More importantly, with 5-5 he would be facing two overcards, so he might be willing to fold to a continuation bet. Your opponent also could have missed the flop with all kinds of hands like middle suited connectors or a weak ace such as A-6.

Since there isn't a strong chance that you are beaten, your best play is to bet about half the pot, or around $2,000, and represent a pair of kings. Hopefully he will lose heart and fold without putting up a fight. After all, you did raise under the gun, so he might put you on A-K, K-Q or K-J. If he raises, you will fold. If he calls, you will not put any more money into the pot on the turn. If he calls your bet on the flop and checks on the turn, he might be playing a small pocket pair or second pair with a hand like A-8 carefully. Nevertheless, you would check again on the river and if he bets, you would probably have to make a tough fold, even though he could be reading for you for a weak hand and is just trying to buy the pot. Once again, remember that you made a minimum raise preflop to keep the pot small and be able to get away from your hand if needed without losing a lot of chips.

PICKING OFF SHORT STACKS

We briefly touched on the importance of avoiding doubling up the short stacks, but it is a point that is worth elaborating upon. I do not recommend trying to pick off the short stacks with almost any two cards like in a Level A sit-and-go, or like many other players in a strong chip position in Level B will try to do. Although eliminating players is useful, wasting chips and extending the game by spreading your chips around the table is highly counterproductive, especially since you need your valuable chips for a top-two finish. Rather than making a questionable call after an opponent puts pressure on you and entices you to risk losing a large pot with a marginal hand, it is much better to wait for a solid hand to pick off a short stack.

The marginal hands that players with large stacks like to play to pick off short stacks with include: A-9 down to A-2; K-Q down to K-9; Q-J, Q-10, J-10, or J-9 suited; sometimes other low suited connectors like 9-8 or 8-7; and any pocket pair. With many of these hands, a player would end up playing:

1. A coin flip;
2. A hand that is dominated;
3. A hand that is behind by about 1.4 to 1, such as K-J vs. A-9, or 8-7 suited vs. A-10;
4. A hand that is ahead by about 1.4 to 1, such as K-9 vs. Q-J.

Considering what is at stake, it is rarely worth risking a large portion of your chips just to satisfy your curiosity about whether or not you have your opponent beat. More than likely, you will just give an opponent an opportunity to double up. Ironically, when a big stack makes a reckless call and gets his money in bad against a short stack, you are rooting for the big stack to suck out and win in order to eliminate an opponent. You don't mind when a player with a solid chip stack wins even more chips, so long as it gets you closer to a top two finish. Although it may be difficult for you to do battle heads-up with this opponent, you at least want to be in a position to work out a deal and walk away with a nice profit.

What if you are facing an all-in bet from a short stack and you are holding a hand that is in the high range of the aforementioned marginal hands, such as A-9, K-Q, or 7-7? You must stop and think about how desperate your opponent is and what he might be holding before considering making a call with these hands. If the short stack has more than five times the opening pot he is not that desperate, so an all-in bet in this situation could still mean he has a strong hand such as a big ace that he doesn't want to play a flop with or maybe pocket tens or nines. If he only has two or three times the opening pot, he might feel that he is forced to move in with any ace, any king, Q-10, Q-9, Q-8, J-10 and any small pair including 2-2. Only then could you consider making the call, but you would still want to make sure it doesn't cost you a large portion of your chip stack, which generally is a bet that is larger than 25 percent of your stack.

KEY TAKEAWAY

When you have a solid chip stack you are in a good position to finish in the top two. Avoid calling all-in bets that are larger than 25 percent of your chip stack when you have a weak hand.

AVOIDANCE IN THE END GAME

Avoidance in the end game is an art form. You might hold a hand with which most players would be willing to put their tournament life on the line. However, by folding you allow your opponents to do battle against each other, which could knock a player out of the tournament and enable you to move closer to the top two.

Here is an example. You are four handed and the blinds are $300/$600 with $100 antes. The chip leader has $11,400, you have $7,100, the next highest chip stack is $5,900, and the shortest stack has $5,600. You are holding Q♦ J♦ on the puck, but the big stack limped in under the gun. Since he acquired his large stack, he has developed a pattern of raising whenever he enters a pot, so you're not sure what to make of his limp. Also, he has shown a tendency to get involved in a pot if an opponent raises from the button, presumably doubting the strength of the raiser's hand.

While you might otherwise raise the pot hoping to at least steal the blinds, you decide to limp in because you want to look at the flop and you don't want to play a big pot against the big stack just yet. You also don't want the big stack to reraise. You will play your hand as a drawing hand, hoping to pick up a lot of outs on the flop if you don't flop at least top pair. After the small blind folds, the big blind who started the hand with $5,900, unexpectedly raises to $2,000. The big stack calls.

SITUATION

You Have: Q♦ J♦
Money in the Pot: $5,300
Bet for You to Call: $1,400
Number of Players: 3

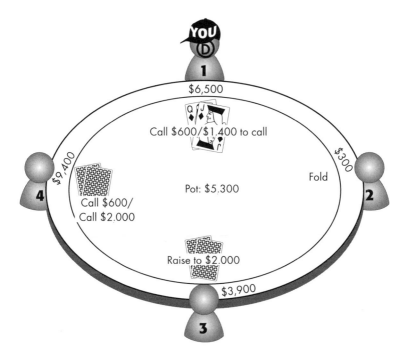

You are getting about 3.8 to 1 on your money, which is very favorable. However, you limped in for a reason. You wanted to see the flop cheaply, knowing that you could fold if you got raised. The problem is that it will cost you a pretty large portion of your remaining stack to call (22 percent), and if you lose the hand and the big blind in Seat 3 wins, you could become the short stack with four players left, which isn't ideal. You know you are holding a hand that doesn't stand up well to a raise unless you think you can move in and get your opponents off their hands, but it is unlikely that you will be able to do that in this situation.

Seat 3 probably isn't making a play at the pot with absolutely nothing, especially since you and the big stack had already entered the pot. In fact, it is surprising that he didn't just move in preflop. It looks like he has a big hand and wants the action. It is hard to know what the chip leader in Seat 4 is holding as he could have a hand like K-J suited, he could have a small pair like sevens, and he also could be playing a speculative hand like 7-6 suited. He limp-called a raise against an opponent that has relatively few chips left. Perhaps he is just hoping for a good flop with any of these hands, and he avoided pushing because he was expecting Seat 3 to call.

In any case, you don't have a very strong hand and you can't just start gambling your chips away with queen-high. Also, there is some upside in folding since you might get to watch Seat 4 eliminate Seat 3, which would leave you in second place with one more player to be eliminated. You decide to fold.

The flop comes J♣ 9♠ 9♥. Seat 3 moves in and Seat 4 calls. Seat 3 turns over K♠ K♣, and Seat 4 turns over a solid hand himself with A♠ J♠. The turn is a blank. But the A♣ on the river eliminates Seat 3. If you had decided to call the raise preflop, you would have flopped two pair, and you would have had a tough decision even with that much action in front of you. Still, you probably would have had to fold considering that Seat 4 called a sizeable bet on the flop worth around 40 percent of his remaining stack.

When you have a lot of chips in the end game, you can afford to look at some flops or to raise and steal a few blinds, but you cannot allow yourself to get sucked into larger pots with marginal hands against the short stacks. Let other players make that mistake, and perhaps you can sit back and watch as your opponents eliminate each other, putting you closer to a top-two finish.

WHEN YOU ARE THE SHORT STACK

Having a small chip stack is an unfortunate and challenging position to be in. However, all is not lost even when you have as little as five opening pots left. While you might be tempted to move in preflop with a wide range of hands in a desperate attempt to steal blinds or perhaps to get lucky and double up, you will still play a short stack strategically and in a way that will serve your end goal of a top two finish. You will not rely completely on luck and just accept any coin flip situation (or worse) that might present itself. Depending on how low your chip stack is, you will still wait for a reasonably strong hand with which to move in. And if you are put to a decision by someone who raises in front of you, your hand requirements will tighten up even more.

The reason you don't want to panic and get all your money in with any type of hand is that second place is extremely valuable. You can benefit by folding and letting your opponents face off against each other even when you are running out of time and chips. If other players at the table are in a similar position as you, there is no legitimate reason for you to play desperately. It will benefit you to fold weak hands and wait to see if a big stack eliminates one or more of your short-stacked opponents. Meanwhile you will wait as long as you can for a hand that gives you a decent chance for a double-up should you get called, because just one double-up could put you in position for a top two finish.

Here is what a table might look like when you are on a short stack.

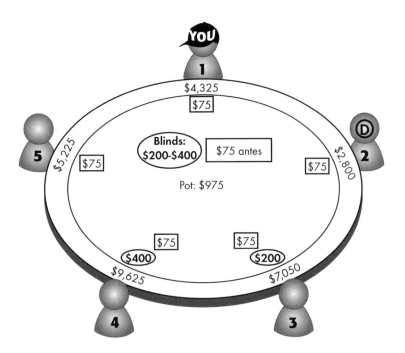

In this situation there are only five players left and blinds and antes are at $200/$400 with $75 antes. You have about four and a half opening pots, while the player in Seat 2 only has about three left, so you are both on the short stack. Even the player in Seat 5 has only a little more than five opening pots, so he's pretty much in the same situation.

When you look at the comfortable chip lead the players in seats 3 and 4 have, it is clear that you have two opponents who need to open up their range of starting hands and two who can afford to pick off the short stacks. If your short-stack opponents start moving in too often, or if they move in recklessly with random hands like 9♣ 5♥ or 8♠ 3♣, you will probably get closer to a top-two finish because there is a strong likelihood they will get knocked out. While you certainly don't have time to wait around for hands like pocket aces, kings or queens, you will want to make sure that you enter the pot with hands that give you a decent chance to win and double up. The hands you should play might not all be strong hands, but they won't necessarily be very low percentage hands.

The following is a list of hands with which you can take the lead preflop by going all-in. You will notice that the range of hands changes in accordance with the number of players sitting at the table. Also, the range of hands tightens up if another player has raised in front of you since you will have lost your first mover advantage. Remember that you want to be the one putting your opponents to a tough decision and not vice versa.

HANDS TO BET ALL-IN WHEN YOU ARE THE SHORT STACK

AT A FULL NINE OR TEN-HANDED TABLE

POCKET ACES TO NINES, A-K, A-Q, A-J

At a full table the chances of running into a strong hand is high, so you want to play pretty strong hands yourself. Notice that K-Q does not appear on this list. That is because at a full table you are likely to get called by someone with a decent ace like A-10, so there is a strong chance that you will get your money in when you are behind by about 1.4 to 1, which is not something you want unless you are completely desperate. Also notice that very small pairs are not recommended. Again, players will be looking to pick you off, so you can expect to get called by other small pairs like eights and sevens, and you never want to get your money in when your hand is dominated. Another key reason you should have this tight range of starting hands is that at a full table, the blinds don't come around quickly and eat away at your chip stack like they do when you are shorthanded. Therefore, you have less reason to feel desperate.

If a player raises in front of you, your range of starting hands with which to move in becomes A-A, K-K, Q-Q, J-J and 10-10; and A-K or A-Q. Remember that if you are short-stacked this early in the tournament, and especially in the first blind level, your opponents will often be raising with solid hands, so you need strong hands with which to double up.

AT A FIVE OR SIX-HANDED TABLE

POCKET ACES TO SEVENS, A-K TO A-10, K-Q, K-J

Notice that this range of hands does not open up to a large degree compared to that at a full table. Since second place is desirable, you do not want to start taking on huge risk by moving in with hands like A-5 because you might get called by players holding bigger aces or pocket pairs higher than fives. Remember that your opponents are looking to build their chip stacks while also trying to eliminate you, so you will want to surprise them by getting your money in with a stronger hand than they are expecting. If a player raises in front of you, your range of starting hands with which to move in becomes pocket aces through pocket nines, A-K, A-Q, or A-J. Do not come over the top with king-high.

AT A THREE OR FOUR-HANDED TABLE

POCKET ACES TO FIVES, A-K TO A-7, K-Q TO K-9 SUITED, Q-J, Q-10 SUITED, AND SMALL SUITED CONNECTORS

Now you can open up your range of starting hands. At such a shorthanded table, there is a much smaller chance that your opponents will hold cards that are strong enough for them to call you, and sometimes they will call with weaker and even dominated hands. The blinds will come around very quickly when the table is this shorthanded, so you will need to embrace risk—if you tighten up too much you will get blinded out.

K-J and K-10 appear on this list because someone playing Q-J or Q-10 might call you, and you would have a decent chance to win the pot if someone calls with a weak ace like A-6. When you play hands like queen-high and small suited connectors such as 7♣ 6♣, you certainly don't want to get called because you will almost never be winning. However, a lot of the time your opponents will fold and you will win the blinds. If you get called with these hands, hopefully your cards will be live and still give you a chance to win. For example, if you are playing 7♠ 5♠, sometimes you will be up against two overcards like A-J and you won't be in terrible shape since you would only be behind by about 1.5 to 1. However, the real problem develops when someone with an overpair calls you. Your 7♠ 5♠ is behind by about 3.7 to 1 against J-J, for example. By comparison, if you play A-10 and a high pair such as Q-Q calls, you would be behind by about 2.4 to 1, so you would stand a substantially better chance of winning than if you were holding a suited connector.

Keeping the danger of playing suited connectors in mind, always remember the important factor here is that you remain alive. For this reason, you must not move in twice in a row with the weaker hands. For example, if you have just won the blinds by moving in with K-J, it is best to muck suited connectors on the next hand. What you want to do is make it look like you wait for solid hands with which to push; if you become too active, your opponents will start calling you down. You don't want to get knocked out of the tournament when you are so close to achieving your objective of playing a heads-up match. You will have to play your short stack aggressively yet somewhat vigilantly, meaning that you will always need to assess your opponents' behavior, your table image, and the likelihood of getting called.

If a player raises in front of you, your range of starting hands with which to move in three or four-handed action becomes pocket aces to eights, and A-K to A-10. This smaller range will give you a good chance to put your tournament on the line as a favorite.

PLAYING ON THE BUBBLE

Here is one final and very important point regarding three-handed play. Playing three-handed means that you are on the bubble, just one spot away from your pot of gold. While you need to be active to avoid getting blinded out, you really need to play a balanced short-stack game and show a little patience. Why? Because if your two opponents start battling each other, one of them could get eliminated and you will finish in the top two. Another possibility is that the chip leader makes a mistake or gets unlucky and he loses a lot of his chips.

You should stay very aware of how your opponents are playing—and you should also be self-aware, paying close attention to how often you are moving in. Your timing is critical, as every decision and move you make could be your last. Avoid moving in twice in a row unless your second hand is strong. And when you are stealing the blinds, try to move in on the big blind occupied by the opponent that you think is playing a little tighter.

Anytime you think there is a high likelihood of getting called when you have only a few opening pots left, it is better to fold trash hands like 9♣ 4♠ and wait to pick up a face card. Moving in with Q♣ 10♠ is way better than moving in with 9♣ 4♠ because if you get called with 9♣ 4♠, you will likely be up against two overcards or an overpair. With a face card in your hand, you could be in a 40/60 situation, or behind by 1.5 to 1, such as Q♣ 10♠ against A♦ J♥. With two trash undercards like 9♣ 4♠, you would be about a 32/68 underdog against A♦ J♥, or behind by more than 2 to 1.

Your objective when you are shorthanded is to steal a few pots so that you can remain alive long enough to double up with a solid hand. In order to meet this objective, you shouldn't push so frequently that your opponents start calling you down with hands they would otherwise fold if you were a little more patient. When your timing is on, you will successfully persuade opponents that you have been waiting around for strong hands such as A-Q, A-J and 10-10. As a result, you will get opponents to fold an ace with a very weak kicker, or small pairs such as 4-4 and 3-3 when you are sometimes holding a vulnerable hand. Eventually, with a little luck you will double against an opponent who calls you down with a hand that you are beating.

Now let's dissect and discuss some live action hands to further your understanding of the strategies and skills you need to win your next big-money sit-and-go satellite.

9 SIT-AND-GO ACTION HANDS

ACTION HAND #1

Five minutes into a Level A sit-and-go, the blinds are $25/$50. At a full table, you have Q♦ Q♣ in middle position. A seemingly aggressive player in Seat 8 raises under the gun to $150 and you reraise to $450. Seat 6 on the button calls. The initial raiser moves in, and he has you covered.

SITUATION

Blinds/Antes: $25/$50
You Have: Q♦ Q♣
Money in the Pot: $2,175
Bet for You to Call: $750
Number of Players: 3

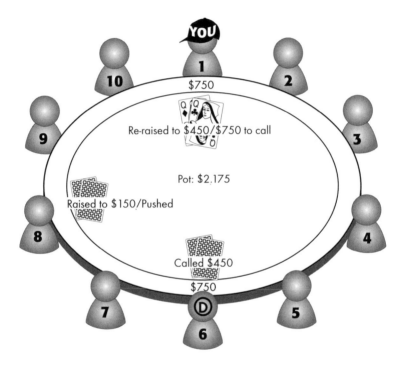

Judging from the first five minutes of the game you have a feeling that Seat 8 is an aggressive player and you do not want to risk folding the best hand in a Level A sit-and-go. He could be playing A-K, so you would be in a coin flip situation, which isn't great but isn't a disaster either considering that you are getting almost 3 to 1 on your money. Of course, he could also be on a lower pair like jacks, tens or nines. There is even a small chance he is just trying to represent aces and he in fact has a hand like J-10 suited. As for Seat 6, he could have a hand like pocket jacks, tens or nines, or A-K, A-Q or A-J, with a small chance that he is slow playing pocket aces or kings.

Definitely call in this situation. If either opponent has pocket aces or kings, then so be it. Just sign up for another Level A sit-and-go if you don't suck out. However, your opponents probably know that a short-stacked sit-and-go can be a bit of a crapshoot, so they could easily be overplaying hands you are beating. If you are right and your hand holds up, you could triple up.

You call. Seat 6 takes his time, says "What the hell!" and calls. He turns over 5♥ 5♣, and Seat 8 turns over A♠ Q♠. Your hand holds up and you triple up early. Seat 6 must have known he was beaten, but was just trying to get lucky, and Seat 8 simply overplayed his hand trying to represent aces or kings.

ACTION HAND #2

In a Level A sit-and-go, you have $2,100 in chips and the blinds are at $50/$100. There are seven players left. You are on the button with K♣ J♣, and there are two limpers in front of you. You decide to raise to $300 instead of just looking at the flop. If you get one caller, you plan to represent a big hand and bet the flop almost regardless of what comes off.

You only get one caller, a player to your immediate right in the cutoff position. This is good news since, if he initially couldn't raise with his hand in the cutoff position, he is probably on a low pair and is looking to flop a set, or he is playing a speculative hand like a suited connector. You are looking for a ragged flop with at least one face card, which would probably enable you to make a successful continuation net.

The flop comes 8♦ Q♦ 3♥. He checks, and you bet $450 into the pot of $850. You are hoping he doesn't have a queen, an 8, or pocket nines, because with these hands he would either call or check-raise you. You aren't putting him on pocket jacks or tens because he probably would have raised preflop with those hands. Alas, he folds.

ACTION HAND #3

It is late in a Level A sit-and-go. Blinds are $200/$400 with $75 antes. There are three players left so the opening pot is $825. You are on the button (which also happens to be under the gun) with K♥ 9♦. You have $5,725 left in chips, the player in the small blind has $3,725, and the short stack in the big blind has $1,725.

You are looking to knock out the short stack. You want to be the one to do it instead of your opponent in the small blind because doing so would give you better than a 2 to 1 chip lead over him heads-up. You also know that with blinds and antes this high, you could lose your chip lead if you start playing too tight and letting your opponents pick up too many opening pots. At the very least you would like to win the blinds and antes.

SITUATION

Blinds/Antes: $200/$400 with $75 antes
You Have: K♥ 9♦
Money in the Pot: $825
Number of Players: 3

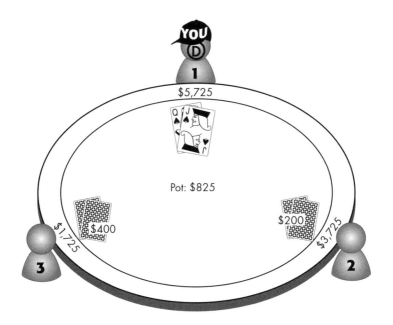

You decide to raise to $1,000 knowing full well that the short stack in the big blind might move in with any half-decent hand because he will soon be out of chips and he is invested in this pot. However, if he has a real trash hand like 8-4 or 10-3, he will probably muck it. Also, it will cost the small blind another $800 to call, which is still a significant portion of his chip stack (21 percent), so he would need a pretty good hand to call or move in.

The small blind folds and the big blind moves in for another $1,125 on top. There is now $3,550 in the pot, so you are getting better than 3 to 1 on your money. This is an easy call for you because, even if your hand is dominated by a hand such as A-K or K-Q, you are still getting the right price to call. More likely is that you have live cards, which makes calling that much more correct. Also, even if you lose this pot, you will still have $3,600 in chips, which is enough to compete.

You call and your opponent turns over A♣ 7♥. He has a stronger hand than you would have expected in the big blind three-handed, but you are only about a 1.4 to 1 underdog so you were certainly getting the right price to call. The board comes 8♣ 8♠ 9♣ J♣ 5♦, and you knock out your opponent with your two pair. You now prepare to play heads-up with a solid chip lead.

ACTION HAND #4

In a Level A sit-and-go, you pick up 6♥ 5♥ under the gun. There are seven players left and the blinds are $50/$100. You have $1,900 in chips. You want to play your hand but if you limp in, you could face a big raise, which would mean you could no longer play your hand cheaply. You would probably have to fold if someone raised to $400 or $500 behind you because you would lose an opportunity to take the lead in the hand and control the pot.

You decide to make a blocking bet by raising to $275. By doing this, you are representing a big hand since you are under the gun; therefore, only strong hands like pocket nines or higher, or A-K or A-Q could reraise you. Players holding hands like A-J, A-10, K-Q or pocket eights would probably just call. To your surprise you get four callers.

SITUATION

Blinds/Antes: $50/$100
You Have: 6♥ 5♥
The Board: 9♥ 6♣ A♥
Money in the Pot: $1,425
Number of Players: 5

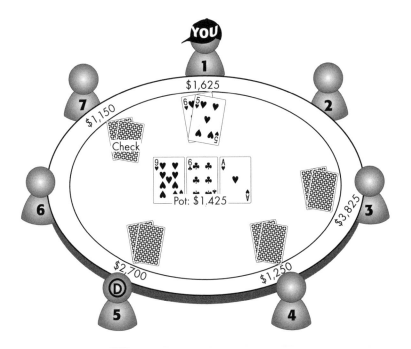

You have flopped a pair and a flush draw. The big blind checks to you. Although you might not be holding the winning hand right now, this is still the kind of flop you are looking for, so you are willing to go to war with it, especially since there are a lot of chips in the pot. What you like about your hand is that if someone is playing A-J or A-10, for example, you have as many as fourteen outs to improve and win a potentially huge pot. In fact, with that many outs and two cards to come, you are winning mathematically and that is why you are willing to bet all your chips in this situation.

There is also a small chance that everyone will fold if you bet or check-raise here because, as preflop raiser, you would be representing a hand like A-K or A-Q. You would just have to hope that someone isn't playing pocket nines or sixes, A-9, A-6 or 9-6, because your number of outs would be reduced by at least three and as many as five. However, even if you cannot win by hitting two pair or trip sixes, you would still have as many as nine outs to hit your flush, which means that the worst-case scenario is that you are behind by about 1.8 to 1, which is not disastrous.

Knowing there is a good chance someone has paired his ace, and since you want to exert maximum pressure with this type of hand, you decide to check-raise. Also, if it just so happens that nobody bets the flop, you would get a free look at the turn with about a 28 percent chance to improve your hand, which isn't a bad turn of events either.

After you check, the chip leader in Seat 3 bets out $750, which is about half the pot. Everyone folds around to you. Now what? You move in and he rolls his eyes as he pushes all his chips in the middle and says, "I should have reraised preflop." He turns over A♦ Q♠. It seems he wanted to play his chip lead conservatively preflop so he just called to look at the flop first before committing more chips. The turn card is the 4♣ and the river card is the 10♥, so you win a $4,675 pot with your flush and take over the chip lead at the table. You now have almost 40 percent of all the chips in play with seven players left, a terrific lead.

ACTION HAND #5

In a Level B sit-and-go where starting chips are $3,000, you are in the first level of blinds ($25/$50) holding A♠ 10♠ in the big blind. Four players limp in and the action is on the player in the small blind, who raises to $250.

SITUATION

Blinds/Antes: $25/$50
You Have: A♠ 10♠
Money in the Pot: $500
Bet for You to Call: $200
Number of Players: 6

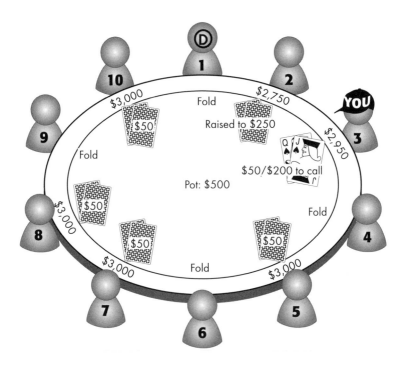

While you know that you are probably beaten, you would like to see the flop to determine whether you flop a draw to the nut flush or perhaps flop two pair or trip tens. Maybe you will be ahead on a 10-high flop.

Despite your desire to play your hand, fold! It is too early in the tournament to start playing raised pots with A-10, especially in this spot where you are more than likely beaten by a bigger ace or maybe even a big pair like kings. Even if he is making a move with a small pocket pair such as eights or nines, your disadvantage looking at the flop is about 2 to 1, since you only have about a 32 percent chance of pairing one of your hole cards on the flop. While you do have the chips to gamble and look at the flop, the small blind's raise is still sizeable (5x the big blind) and in this sit-and-go, you can run out of chips quickly if you start taking too many gambles. In addition, while you would hope to pick up a nice draw on the flop, you would still have to spend more money to potentially draw out on someone. Finally, there are four other players yet to act behind you and you are holding a hand that cannot withstand a reraise in case someone in early position is sandbagging a solid pair or A-K.

ACTION HAND #6

At $25/$50 in a Level B sit-and-go, a player raises to $175 in middle position and it is folded around to you on the button. You are holding J♣ J♥. There is one limper in early position.

There are two feasible options for you here. One is to just call, look at the flop, and hope there are no overcards on board. If there are no overcards, you can bet or raise hoping to take it down on the flop. One problem with this option is that it is early in the tournament and most players are still deep in chips; therefore, there could be a few callers behind you, especially after you give them pot odds by calling. This means that even if there are no overcards on the flop, you still risk playing a big pot against someone who might hit the flop really big or who is perhaps on a big draw. Also, if there is just one overcard in a three or four-way pot, there is a strong chance someone has you beaten, so you couldn't really fire a bet on the flop to try to take it down. Despite seeming safe at first, this option isn't actually a great one.

The second option is to reraise, which is the option I recommend. You don't have to make a large bet, but by reraising to an amount like $450, you would make it much more difficult for anyone else to call behind you and you would isolate the initial raiser. While a small reraise might show weakness and entice your opponent to come over the top, it is still better than overplaying pocket jacks by reraising to an amount such as $600 or $700. However, after you reraise, if your opponent comes over the top with a third raise, assume that you are beaten or are at best up against A-K, and fold. You don't want to commit all your chips preflop with jacks this early in level B.

If he just calls your reraise and an ace, king or queen hit the flop, fire a $500 bet if he checks to you, since he might have missed and you could represent A-K or A-Q. Also, if he is holding pocket queens and he only called your reraise preflop to make sure there were no overcards, he might give it up if there is an ace or king on the flop. If there are no overcards on the flop and your opponent is still giving you action, assume that he made a tricky call preflop with pocket aces, kings or queens, and fold. Even if he gives you action on a 10-high flop, it is doubtful he is playing A-10, so assume that you are beaten.

In the first blind level, don't risk your entire tournament by overplaying pocket jacks. Thin the field in order to play the pot heads-up, and avoid a situation where you might find yourself locked in and committed to the pot when you are beaten.

ACTION HAND #7

It is relatively early in a Level B sit-and-go, and you have built up your chip stack to $4,900 by winning two medium sized pots with strong hands. It is now halfway through the second blind level ($50/$100) and you think it might be time to start taking advantage of the tight image that you created showing down premium hands. You decide to keep your eyes open for opportunities to steal a pot or two.

The table has loosened up a little and players are starting to raise pots and call raises with marginal aces, K-Q, K-J, K-10 suited, K-9 suited, some low connecting cards, and low pocket pairs.

You are sitting one seat to the right of the cutoff position, which is often referred to as the hijack, holding 10♦ 8♥. In front of you, an average-tight player in middle position raises to $300, and a weak-tight player to his left calls. The weak-tight player isn't short stacked, but he has only $1,900 left and you've noticed that he has limp-folded a few times preflop. The action comes to you.

SITUATION

Blinds/Antes: $50/$100
You Have: 10♦ 8♥
Money in the Pot: $750
Bet for You to Call: $300
Number of Players: 7

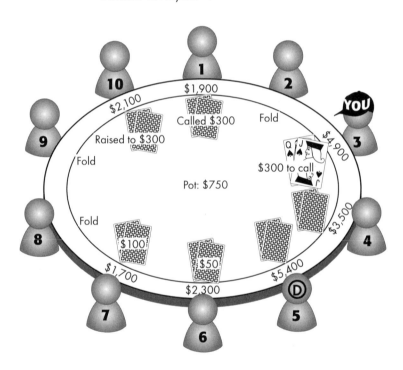

It feels like the raiser might be holding a hand that he can fold—A-J, A-10, K-Q, K-J or a pair like pocket nines. As for the caller, you don't think he has a strong hand since he didn't reraise. He just seems to be playing soft poker, meaning that you can bully him.

You decide to represent pocket aces, kings or queens by reraising to $1,000 in the hope that everyone folds. You are betting $1,000 to win $750 so the risk-reward scenario seems favorable. Also, you are raising two opponents instead of just one, which makes it seem like it would be a risky time to bluff. You are also sitting next to the cutoff instead of on the button, so your bet might not appear to be just a position raise. Also, you have a lot of chips and you have your opponents covered, so they probably want to make sure they have a strong hand before they get involved in a big pot with you. Finally, the only hands you've showed down in big pots are strong hands, so your tight image might persuade everyone to fold.

Even if someone comes over the top and you have to fold, or if someone calls and the action is such that you are unable to put more money into the pot after the flop, you will still have a competitive chip stack of $3,900.

Sure enough, everyone folds and you grow your chip stack to $5,650. What a player!

ACTION HAND #8

It is deep into the third blind level ($100/$200) of a Level B sit-and-go. You have been completely card dead. Further, you got unlucky the one time you got your money into a significant pot. In that hand a short stack that was trailing you by about 4 to 1 hit his five-outer and doubled through you. You are now the shortest stack at the table with $1,600 in chips and seven players left.

You have a little more than five times the opening pot, so you are starting to get low in chips but you are not desperate yet. However, if your chip count continues to drop, you will have so few chips that you will not be able to steal any pots, as your all-in bets would certainly get called by players with larger stacks who are looking to eliminate you. Also, the next blind level ($100/$200 with $25 antes) begins in about three minutes, at which point you will have roughly three and a half times the opening pot, since the pots will increase by $175 to $475.

You are sitting in the hijack. There are two limpers in front of you, one of whom is under the gun. The other limper is second in chips with $4,700. The action comes to you, holding A♦ 8♣.

SITUATION

Blinds/Antes: $100/$200
You Have: A♦ 8♣
Money in the Pot: $700
Bet for You to Call: $200
Number of Players: 7

This is not a terrible hand, but it isn't a very good hand either. At an eight-handed table there is a pretty good chance someone else is holding an ace, and most of your opponents can afford to risk calling a short stack's all-in bet with a weak or middle ace like A-9, A-10 or A-J. Furthermore, a couple of players have at least shown interest in their hands, and one of them has a lot of chips. Since they are in early position, one of them could also be slow-playing a big hand. In addition, there are four players behind you to worry about. In short, an all-in move here is a little too dangerous.

You decide to fold. Even though going all-in would still be a large opening bet for your opponents to call, your hand is just too marginal to throw caution to the wind right now. Remember, there is an important element of survival in this sit-and-go. You must make sure that you don't get knocked out before being able to make a deal or at least before the weaker players are eliminated. What you want to do is wait for a hand that will give you a good chance to double up—A♦ 8♣ is not one of those hands.

If you had picked up a bigger ace like A-J, you would have moved in and hoped to get called by a weaker hand, win a coin flip, or just win the pot right there. If the table had been three or four-handed and nobody had limped in front of you, moving in with A♦ 8♣ would have been a good play.

ACTION HAND #9

It is late in a Level B sit-and-go. The blinds and antes are $300/$600 with $100 antes. Four players are left. The chip leader has $12,000, the player with the next largest stack has $7,400, you have $6,800 and the short stack has $3,800. The table has been playing very fast, as it is the day before the first Day 1 of a WPT tournament and everyone is feeling the pressure to win a seat. The two players in the chip lead have also shown the capacity to play back at each other, so they are not just waiting around passively for the short stack to get blinded out. They want more chips!

You are holding 6♠ 6♦ on the button. The player with $7,400 is sitting to your immediate right and limps in under the gun. You also decide to limp in to see if you can flop a set. The chip leader is in the big blind so you don't want to raise with a marginal hand like sixes in case he reraises because you would have to lay your hand down. You also don't want to put your whole tournament on the line by shoving with pocket sixes because you are not short-stacked, so you have time to wait for a stronger hand to push with preflop. You realize that these two chip leaders are looking for opportunities to add to their chip stacks.

The small blind also calls and the chip leader checks in the big blind, so it is a family pot. The flop comes 9♥ 6♣ 10♥. You have flopped bottom set. To your delight, the short stack moves in for $3,400. However, the chip leader calls and the other player also calls.

SITUATION

Blinds/Antes: $300/$600 with $100 antes
You Have: 6♠ 6♦
The Board: 9♥ 6♣ 10♥
Bet for You to Call: $3,400
Money in the Pot: $13,000
Number of Players: 4

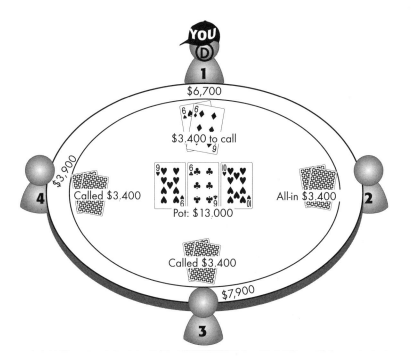

Whoa! What just happened here? You now have a very tough decision to make, by far the most important one you will make in this sit-and-go. You are holding the fourth-best possible hand on this flop, and probably the second-best hand in actuality since it is likely that someone would have raised preflop with 10-10 or 9-9. Most likely, only someone holding 8-7 is beating you right now with a straight. However, there is a very good chance you are up against at least one player who is drawing to a hand that can beat your set. There is a long list of hand combinations that you could be up against, including a number of flush draw/straight draw combinations—and you don't have a big edge over those hands.

The toughest part about this situation is that if you get involved, it will be for all your chips since it is costing you about half your remaining stack to call this bet, yet you probably don't have your opponents crushed. Your opponents will almost certainly put you all-in on the flop because they have invested so many of their chips already; you cannot call and expect them to check it down. However, if you win the hand, you will have a huge chip lead and be in an excellent position to win the sit-and-go.

Despite the opportunity to win it all, you must remember that your objective is to finish in the top two. The reality is that you are in a situation where you could get knocked out when you have an opportunity to fold and let your opponents knock each other out. It is possible that the chip leader in Seat 3 will knock out both of his opponents and you will achieve your goal of playing heads-up just by getting out of the way and folding. It is also possible that Seat 4 will win this huge pot, knock out Seat 2 and cripple Seat 3, which would put you second in chips with three players left.

Your decision is either to fold and move closer to a top-two finish, or risk getting knocked out. What to do? Even though you are probably holding the best hand right now, you should fold.

Letting your opponents play off each other is the best decision here. You are probably up against a large number of outs with an outside chance that you are already beaten by 8-7. All of your opponents have just committed a large portion of their chip stacks to this pot, so it is highly unlikely that they are merely holding a hand like top pair. Calling is very risky here when you could simply fold and still end up with a better chance to finish in the top two than you had before the hand started.

After you fold, the action continues. The turn card is the K♦, so the board is 9♥ 6♣ 10♥ K♦. Seat 3 checks and Seat 4 moves in. Seat 3 calls and turns over the nuts with Q♥ J♥, with an opportunity to improve to a straight flush. The short stack in Seat 2 turns over 4♥ 3♥, so he has a smaller flush draw. Seat

4 turns over 10♦ 9♣, which gives him top two pair, and wins the pot with a full house after the 9♠ shows up on the river.

You would have been knocked out of the tournament had you called with your set. Instead, the table is now three-handed and you are second in chips. If Seat 4 hadn't hit his four-outer, you would be negotiating a deal heads-up with Seat 3.

ACTION HAND #10

In the middle stage of a Level B sit-and-go, the blinds and antes are $150/$300 with $50 antes. Six players are left. You are third in chips with $5,100. A well-known tournament professional is playing at your table. Huck Seed won the World Series of Poker Main Event as a very young man in 1996, and made the final table again in 1999. Most players at the table seem a little distracted with him there, as they keep looking to him for approval after they win a pot. They keep talking to him in order to get chummy with him. A player in the cutoff position points to you and says, "I am going to bluff you, my friend," and he looks over at the poker celebrity to see if he is watching.

A few hands later you are in the big blind with 3♣ 2♦. Two players limp in, including the player who called you out. The small blind folds and you check. There are three players in the hand. The flop comes 6♦ 10♣ 10♠. You check, Seat 3 checks, and Seat 4 (the player who said he intends to bluff you) bets $400 into the $750 pot.

SITUATION

Blinds/Antes: $150/$300 with $50 antes
You Have: 3♣ 2♦
The Board: 6♦ 10♣ 10♠
Bet for You to Call: $400
Money in the Pot: $1,150
Number of Players: 3

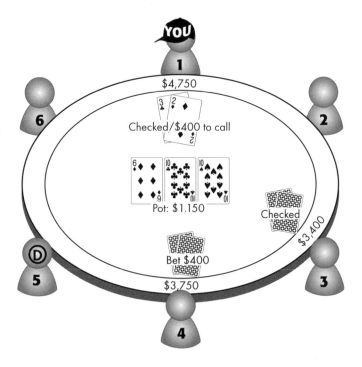

Seat 4 might be choosing this moment to win the pot in position with nothing and turn over his cards to show everyone (especially Huck) that he bluffed you. Of course, he could also have a 6 in his hand or a small pocket pair likes fours. You decide to try to turn the tables on him by representing a 10 with a bluff-call. You want to be a little deliberate with your action, so you ask the dealer, "How much is that, $400? I call," and you wave the $400 in chips at the dealer before placing them into the pot. Your opponent shifts in his seat. Seat 3 folds behind you.

The turn card is the Q♦, so the board is 6♦ 10♣ 10♠ Q♦. You like the queen because if your opponent has a 6 or a low pocket pair, it is another overcard for him to worry about. There is $1,550 in the pot. You come out betting $700 looking like you are both value betting and defending your trip tens from a possible straight draw or flush draw. Seat 4 folds and you turn over your 3♣ 2♦. The pro laughs heartily and exclaims, "Ha, he caught you with a bluff-call. Nice!" Seat 4 shamefacedly nods.

Yes, you can still have fun playing these sit-and-goes, even though there is a lot of money on the line! With $3,000 starting chips, there is some room for interesting play so you can afford to take some risks and make some moves. Of course, if Seat 4 had started playing back at you in this hand, you would have played it safe and avoided putting any more money in the pot. Your objective is always to finish in the top two—where you can really have fun winning money—and you were already well on your way, so there was no need to get carried away.

Now that we've examined the play of hands, let's move forward to what can happen when you make it to the final two. The next chapter shows you how to master the science of deal making.

10 THE SCIENCE OF THE DEAL

When most poker players buy into tournament satellites such as those for the World Poker Tour, the European Poker Tour or the World Series of Poker, their objective is to win a seat into the Main Event. As you know by now, you don't actually need to cash in the Main Event or even play in it to make a lot of money. You can make excellent profit simply by negotiating a deal in a satellite to ensure that your heads-up match ends prematurely. When it does, it guarantees that you will walk away from the poker table as a big winner.

Making deals or "chops" in satellites is a great way to generate cash profit. Whether you are the chip leader or behind in the chip count heads-up, there is usually a logical reason for the remaining two players to exchange cash in order to end the heads-up match, usually before it even begins. The rationale is that the chip leader is close enough to owning a valuable big buy-in Main Event seat that he will want to prevent his opponent from making a comeback by getting lucky or by outplaying him. The player who is behind in the chip count realizes he might need to get lucky to win. Therefore, the player who is behind concedes first place to the chip leader and receives a cash payoff from him for doing so. The runner up also receives a free replay into another satellite, so he makes a profit while getting to play it again for free.

Of course, this all depends on the players' priorities and their chip counts. It is quite possible that a 5 to 1 chip leader is unwilling to make a deal, or that a player who is behind in chips refuses to accept a deal because he really wants to win the seat outright. Still, players are able to come to an agreement almost every time. With a $10,000 seat on the line, even a strong chip leader will usually agree to pay out some cash to end the match and collect the seat.

CONCESSION ODDS

Concession odds is a tool that you can use to fairly split the prize pool of a tournament when you are heads-up. This tool serves as a guide for knowing the percentage of the prize money you should receive when arranging a chop. What makes this tool valuable is that it takes into consideration the difference in skill level between you and your opponent, as well as the size of your chip stacks. Specifically, concession odds tell you how much more than your fair share of the prize pool you should get against a weaker opponent, and how much less than your fair share you should get against a stronger opponent.

The best part about this tool is that it is very easy to use. In order to simplify your decision making when evaluating chip stacks and the relative difference in skill level between you and your opponent, I recommend using a concession factor of 0.15 (or 15 percent). This is the percentage by which you will make adjustments to the prize splits when you propose a deal. If your opponent is a weaker player, try to negotiate for 15 percent more than your fair share of the prize money. If your opponent is a stronger player, be willing to accept 15 percent less than your fair share of the prize money.

The reason 15 percent works well is that it prevents you from deviating too far from a fair split based on a chip count. The concession factor balances skill level, chip count, and the value of playing out the match, making it a great tool to facilitate your decision making when you are ready to negotiate a deal. While you want to get what you deserve based on relative skill level, you still need to get a deal done, and a 0.15 concession factor will ensure that you propose reasonable numbers to your opponents.

Implicit in the concession factor is your option of playing out the match and winning the Main Event seat outright in case an opponent is not amenable to your offers. Whether you are the chip leader or behind in chips, the option of playing out the match has some value. The concession factor will account for this and ensure that you don't give too much away in your negotiations.

> ### THE CONCESSION FACTOR:
> The percentage by which you will make adjustments to the prize splits when you propose a deal. You want 15% more than your fair share against a weaker player, and you are willing to accept 15% less than your fair share against a stronger player.

Here is an example of using the concession factor. Let's say that you have a 3 to 1 chip lead in a Level B satellite for a $10,300 buy-in tournament. You decide that you want to end the match by offering your opponent a deal. Your opponent is a strong player. According to the chip count, you should receive $7,725 (or 75 percent of the $10,300 prize pool). However, with the use of the calculator function on your mobile phone, you apply the 15 percent concession factor to the $7,725, which shows that you would accept $1,159 less than this ($7,725 x 0.15 = $1,159), which is $6,566 or about $6,600.

Of course, this doesn't mean that your first offer should be $3,700, which is your opponent's share of the $10,300 prize pool after applying the concession factor. Start off by offering your opponent $2,500 or even $2,000. However, if he insists on more and you get into heavy negotiations, at least you will know that the most you are willing to pay him to end the match with a 3 to 1 chip lead is $3,700.

Below you will find concession tables that show what the concession odds and concession dollars are after applying the 0.15 factor against average, stronger, and weaker opponents. These tables are for a Level B sit-and-go with $10,300 in the prize pool.

One factor that is not accounted for in these tables is how high the blinds are. Occasionally, the sit-and-go will take a long time to play out. As a result, the blinds will be so high when you are heads-up that the only plays will be to move all-in preflop. You might think this would encourage some opponents to take their chances and play out the match. In my experience this has not been the case. Chip leaders want to negotiate a deal to prevent you from forcing them to make a big decision or to avoid relying on luck to win. When you also consider that the majority of the time there will be room for play after the flop, you can see that the overall impact of the blinds is small. Therefore, the only relevant factors that need to be accounted for are skill level and chip stacks.

CONCESSION ODDS

0.15 factor for $10,300 prize pool

	YOUR CHIP COUNT							
	AHEAD							
	1.5 to 1	2 to 1	3 to 1	4 to 1	5 to 1	6 to 1	7 to 1	8 to 1
Average Opponent	1.5	2	3	4	5	6	7	8
Stronger Opponent	1.0	1.3	1.8	2.1	2.4	X	X	X
Weaker Opponent	2.2	3.3	6.2	11.5	22.8	X	X	X

	YOUR CHIP COUNT							
	BEHIND							
	1.5 to 1	2 to 1	3 to 1	4 to 1	5 to 1	6 to 1	7 to 1	8 to 1
Average Opponent	1.5	2	3	4	5	6	7	8
Stronger Opponent	1.9	2.5	3.7	4.9	6.0	X	X	X
Weaker Opponent	1.2	1.6	2.5	3.3	4.2	X	X	X

CONCESSION DOLLARS
0.15 factor for $10,300 prize pool

	YOUR CHIP COUNT							
	AHEAD							
	1.5 to 1	2 to 1	3 to 1	4 to 1	5 to 1	6 to 1	7 to 1	8 to 1
Average Opponent	$6,180	$6,850	$7,720	$8,240	$8,580	$8,830	$9,010	$9,245
Stronger Opponent	$5,253	$5,823	$6,562	$7,004	$7,293	X	X	X
Weaker Opponent	$7,107	$7,878	$8,878	$9,476	$9,867	X	X	X

	YOUR CHIP COUNT							
	BEHIND							
	1.5 to 1	2 to 1	3 to 1	4 to 1	5 to 1	6 to 1	7 to 1	8 to 1
Average Opponent	$4,120	$3,450	$2,580	$2,060	$1,720	$1,470	$1,290	$1,055
Stronger Opponent	$3,502	$2,933	$2,193	$1,751	$1,462	X	X	X
Weaker Opponent	$4,738	$3,967	$2,967	$2,369	$1,978	X	X	X

WHAT CAN YOU LEARN FROM THESE TABLES?

WHEN YOU'RE AHEAD AGAINST A WEAK PLAYER

There are some interesting insights that we can glean from these tables. Looking at the first table, you will notice that when you have a large chip lead against a weaker opponent, the odds at which you would accept a deal are astronomically high. For example, when you have a 3 to 1 chip lead against a weaker opponent, you should only be willing to make a deal that gives you a 6.2 to 1 share of the prize money. The corresponding dollar amount is shown in the third table, which indicates that your share should be $8,878, so your weaker opponent's share should be $1,422 ($10,300 - $8,878 = $1,422). These odds are telling you that since you are so close to winning the $10,300 seat outright, your weaker opponent should be willing to take whatever scraps you are willing to give him; otherwise, you will just play out the match and he will risk being left with nothing other than a free replay if he loses.

In reality, most players know when they are up against a tough opponent. When they realize that they are at a big disadvantage in skill and chip count, they are happy to accept over $1,000 to concede first place to you, and then try their luck again for free in another Level B sit-and-go.

WHEN YOU'RE AHEAD AGAINST A STRONGER PLAYER

Now let's look at when you are ahead against a stronger player. Notice that even when you are ahead in chips by as much as 4 to 1 or 5 to 1, you are still willing to offer very enticing odds compared to what you would offer an average player. This makes sense since you can't count as much on a strong opponent making a mistake to help you finish off the match. Also, it only takes one double up or a few consecutive small pots for your opponent to stage a comeback—and a strong player will know how to win more than his fair share of pots after he starts to accumulate chips.

Take a look at the third table (concession dollars when you are ahead in chips) when you have a 4 to 1 chip lead against a strong opponent. You will see that for about $1,200 more than you would offer an average player, you assure yourself of a $7,000 prize, which is a fair deal against a very good player. In short, it is prudent to get some good money in your pocket against a strong player before he or she has a chance to mount a comeback.

WHEN YOU'RE TRAILING THE CHIP LEADER

Now let's look at when you are trailing the chip leader. Notice that the odds you would accept against stronger and weaker opponents don't seem as extreme as when you are the chip leader. This has to do with how the 0.15 concession factor is applied. Just as we do when you are the chip leader, we apply it to your fair share of the prize pool. We do not apply the concession factor to your opponent's fair share. The result is that the differentials are less dramatic since we're changing the smaller dollar amount in the prize splits. The reason it is appropriate to apply it to your fair share is that you want to know how much you would be willing to accept—not how much you think your opponent should accept.

You will also notice that there are no recommended odds or dollars when you or your opponent have a 6 to 1 chip lead or better. Why? Because when a player has a very big chip lead, he should be willing to gamble on his ability to finish off the match. Even against a better player, there is more value in playing out the match than in taking money out of your pocket with a 6 to 1 chip lead. Of course, if an opponent doubles up and you become only a 2.5 to 1 favorite, reconsider and take a look at what the table recommends at that point.

Apply this same thinking if you are the one at a major chip disadvantage. Not only is it unlikely that you will be able to negotiate a deal when you are so far behind, but there is more value in playing it out and relying on luck to make a comeback than in accepting a very small amount of money to end the match.

Looking at the concession dollars table when you are behind in chips against a stronger player, you will notice that the amount of the deviation from your fair share against an average opponent decreases as your opponent's chip lead gets stronger. This seems paradoxical: You would think that as your opponent's chip stack gets stronger, you should be willing to accept an amount that is increasingly farther from the average. However, you must remember that your option of playing out the sit-and-go still has value. Therefore, even if a strong opponent has a very big chip lead, don't settle for some very small amount of money like $500.

With just a little luck or a brief string of good cards, you could win some chips and be in a much stronger bargaining position if you play it out. With that in mind, notice that in the odds table the deviation does increase. However, it rises in small increments. You would think that as a stronger opponent's chip lead increases, you might be willing to accept increasingly worse splits. But again, the value of playing out the match outweighs the value of giving away all of your share of the prize pool.

SELLING FIRST PLACE

There is another bargaining alternative that we haven't yet discussed. If you happen to be in a real fix for money and you have a slight chip lead over an opponent, you could offer to sell first place to him while you take second place and the free replay. I would only suggest this option if you really need the cash and you don't want to play in the main event. Since it is unlikely that your opponent will want to cough up enough cash to cover his fair share of the prize money based on the chip count (for example, more than half of $10,300), you will need to offer him a reduced price. Perhaps he will be pleased to pay you $4,000 out of his pocket. After all, he is behind in the chip count and you are offering a price that reflects his having the chip lead.

If your opponent likes this sort of deal but refuses to pay you that much in cash, and if you think he is a decent player, you could consider yet another option. You could request even less cash and ask for a percentage of his action in the main event, perhaps 10 percent. This means that you get 10 percent of his total prize money based on how deep he finishes in the main event. The main benefit of agreeing to this type of deal is that it offers you some real upside since if he makes the final table or wins the tournament, you could earn really big money.

Although this type of deal seems risky since it is made between strangers, it is not as uncommon as you might think. Many experienced poker players are quite trustworthy. Nevertheless, you will want to be smart about arranging this type of deal. At the very least, be sure to get his cell phone number and call him right away to make sure it is correct. You can find out which Day 1 he will be playing so that you can track his progress, which is something you can do online for most large professional tournaments. Here is what I mean by referring to Day 1. The casino hosting the tournament usually can't accommodate hundreds or, in the case of the WSOP, thousands of entrants. Therefore, players are assigned separate first days. There could be three, four or even five Day 1's followed by a couple of Day 2's.

A NEGOTIATION SCENARIO

Let's look at a mock negotiation scenario so we can apply what we've learned so far about making deals. You are playing in a Level B $1,240 single-table sit-and-go where the winner gets a Main Event seat for a World Poker Tour tournament that costs $10,300 and the runner-up wins a free replay for another $1,240 sit-and-go.

You won your way into this satellite by winning a Level A $170 satellite after three tries, so you are already doing well because you spent $510 to play a sit-and-go that normally costs $1,240. You don't currently own any other seats for the Main Event, so you are playing to win your first seat.

You are heads-up against another good player, and he has a chip lead of about 4 to 1. You know that this guy really wants to get into the Main Event and, based on his chip count, he's almost there. However, you are also a good player and with a little luck, you could double up and be right back in this thing, or at least that's what you will tell him. You want to get him to agree to pay you cash out of his pocket and you will agree to concede first place and the Main Event seat to him.

Looking at the concession tables, you know you won't accept less than $1,750, so naturally you want to start off by suggesting something higher, like $2,200. After he comes back with an offer of $1,800 and you do a little more haggling, you finally agree on $2,000. This deal gives you a cash profit of $1,490, which includes your $170 sit-and-go costs, and you also get a free replay for this satellite. Meanwhile, it guarantees your opponent a seat into a $10,300 buy-in event for a cost of $2,000 plus his previous sit-and-go costs, so he is probably saving a substantial $7,000 or so to play in the Main Event.

Now let's say you make it to another heads-up match in the next Level B sit-and-go you sign up for, where you have a 2 to1 chip lead over a weaker opponent. You can now make an offer for your opponent to concede first place to you. You will have that $2,000 handy, and since the concession tables tell you not to give him more than $2,422, perhaps you can get him to concede for $2,000, which would guarantee your $10,300 Main Event seat for a total cost of just $510. Of course, you could also choose to forego a deal and just play out this heads-up match so you have a shot at winning your seat while also being up by $1,490. This is a judgment call you will need to make based on your financial objectives and on whether you really feel like battling it out.

Sometimes your opponent's style of heads-up play will convince you to offer him a deal. A weaker player might know he is in for a tough match against you and he might start moving in virtually every hand. This prevents you from outplaying him and letting your poker skills beat him over the course of the match. In this case, you will be exposed to more risk since, without any real information about what cards he is holding, you might have to call him with weaker hands than you would like. There will be more luck and less skill involved in this heads-up match, so lean toward offering him a deal before he has a chance to get lucky and double up.

EXECUTING A DEAL

Let's say you are heads-up in a single-table satellite for a special $5,000 buy-in event at one of your local casinos, and you are outchipped by 3.5 to 1 against a slightly weaker opponent. You decide to offer your opponent a deal, so you pull out your mobile phone to use the calculator function. The first thing you want to do is figure out how to split the $5,000 prize pool according to the current chip count in your heads-up match. After figuring out that your fair share is about $1,100, you multiply this figure by 1.15, which gives you your concession total of $1,265, which is the least you will accept in a deal. You decide to ask for $1,500 from your opponent to concede the first-place finish to him. You explain to him that he will win a $5,000 seat uncontested, and it will cost him only 30 percent of the full price to play in the Main Event.

Now let's assume that your opponent seems interested but he is new to this whole process, so it becomes a simple matter of helping him understand the logistics that are standing in the way of your making your score. Since this player is being asked to hand over a lot of money in order to collect a Main Event seat, you will need to explain to him that you have made these deals many times before. He will need to feel assured that this exchange of money is very common in the world of professional tournaments. Tell him that coming up with the cash is quite easy and you will explain to him how to do it.

To help him understand what to do to close this deal, tell him that he should start by seeing how much cash he has on him. Second, he should go to an ATM and withdraw as much of the remaining $1,500 as he can. Third, assuming he still doesn't have enough cash on him, he should go the cashier's window at the casino and take an advance on his credit card.

This third step might seem jarring to him, since few people use this method to borrow money. Explain to him how this works. He simply needs to make a request for a certain amount of money from the cashier and they will process it for him. It really is the same as buying something with his credit card, although there is a higher interest rate associated with this purchase. His credit card company will also charge him a service fee of close to $100 for doing this, so you must assure him that it is worthwhile since he is still getting his $5,000 seat at a big discount. Perhaps you can even offer to split the cost of the cash advance by agreeing to take $50 less than the price you already agreed to. If he still seems skeptical about the process, ask one of the tournament directors to come over. The tournament director will assure him that this deal-making is common, and by agreeing to a deal he will receive a legitimate voucher for the Main Event, so there is no need for him to be concerned.

In a live satellite, players can negotiate confidently knowing that the likelihood of getting paid and completing the transaction is very high. Usually, the dealer or the tournament director will stop the clock while players negotiate a deal. This is beneficial because blinds and antes are usually so high that players feel they can't afford to stop playing in order to negotiate while the clock is running. The tournament director benefits from the negotiation as he ensures that the match ends quickly so he can free up the table to start another sit-and-go.

Some tournament directors even feel it is their responsibility to oversee this transaction just to make sure nobody gets 'robbed' in their poker room.

At the very least, a tournament director will allow players to get cash from an ATM so they can complete a deal while the clock is stopped.

As a gut reaction an opponent sometimes may turn down your offer. After all, it isn't every day that a stranger asks him to hand over that much money in cash. In addition to letting him know that these deals are very common, you may also need to persuade him that it is a good idea to take his seat now while he can. Let him know that you are an experienced player, that you are more than capable of mounting a comeback, and that he wouldn't want to be so close to winning a Main Event seat only to lose it to a quality opponent who outplays him or who gets really good cards. You could also tell him that your price will start to go up as you win pots and close the chip count gap against him.

SOMETIMES IT'S EASY, BUT NOT ALWAYS

Since a lot depends on your opponent, you will find that it sometimes will be very easy to negotiate and execute a deal and other times it will be more challenging. In the Doyle Brunson World Poker Classic at the Bellagio, a $15,400 buy-in event, I was heads-up in a $1,800 Level B satellite against a weaker player who had a 4 to 1 chip lead over me. According to my calculations using the concession factor, I was supposed to receive no less than $3,565 to concede. To my surprise, my opponent quickly accepted my first offer of $5,000, and he reached into his pocket and threw me one black chip worth $5,000. Clearly, this older gentleman was thrilled to have his chance to play in the Main Event.

In my very next satellite at the Bellagio, I was heads-up against a talented young guy who was quite confident in his skills, and I was behind 5 to 1 in chips. Using the concession factor, I figured out that I was supposed to reduce my fair share of $2,550 to $2,170. I offered to accept $2,500 to concede first place but my opponent refused. When he refused my next offer of $2,200, I decided not to lower my price. We continued to play. I won the next two hands and was behind 4 to 1, at which point he requested the terms of my first offer of $2,500. At 4 to 1, I was supposed to refuse anything less than $2,635, so I insisted on $2,600 and he agreed.

So how much total profit did I make? I had bought directly into the $1,800 Level B satellite because I had arrived in Las Vegas the previous day, which didn't leave me enough time to play the Level A satellites. Nevertheless, my two deals generated $7,600 in revenue, so I had earned a net profit of $5,800 after about six hours of poker playing that day. Also, I still had my free replay, which I went on to use to win my seat in the Main Event.

As you can see, this system really works. I don't think that pros are the only ones who can earn a profit with it. I strongly believe that even an average player can be successful using this approach.

SELLING MAIN EVENT SEATS

Let's say you have studied this book thoroughly, you have successfully implemented the game plan, and after making five trips to your local casino, you have won three seats for the main event of a big-money tournament. If you decide to play in the main event, you will need to sell your two extra seats.

There are a few different ways to obtain cash in exchange for your extra main event seats, and they vary depending on the host casino's rules:

1. Collect cash from the casino's poker room in exchange for your extra seats. For some big-money tournaments, the casinos require you to play your first main event seat but provide cash in exchange for any extra seats you win.

2. Collect tournament chips or lammers to sell to players waiting to sign up for satellites or for the main event. This is how it is done at The World Series of Poker at the Rio in Las Vegas. Players are constantly selling lammers to people who are waiting in line to buy their tournament seat or to buy into a satellite. These lammers are chips that are as good as cash at the Rio.

3. Sell your voucher to another player in exchange for cash. This would only be necessary at a casino poker room that doesn't offer you cash in exchange for your vouchers. Instead, you are allowed to transfer vouchers to other players, who need only sign to them in order to own them.

There are many types of potential buyers for your main event seats. Some are pros and wealthy amateurs who would otherwise just go to the casino cage the day before the main event starts to buy into the event. You can find these buyers just by hanging out around the cage. You can also ask around the poker room to see if people know anyone who wants to buy a seat. Also, some home games run their own tournaments where winners get a main event seat. In these cases, you can sell your extra seats to the people who run the game so that they can give the winning players a voucher on the spot. Other options are advertising via free classifieds on websites like Craigslist or Kijiji, or by using online poker blogs and forum posts.

11 MONEY MANAGEMENT

Before you begin to implement the sit-and-go methods in this book you should know how to manage your money like a professional. Money management means managing the money that you set aside for poker games and managing the profit you generate from playing winning poker. The term money management applies to all financial aspects of being a poker player. Some of these aspects include knowing how much you are willing to risk in a poker game, evaluating the size of the cash games you play in, and even when to set aside money for personal savings outside of your poker bankroll. In this chapter I discuss how to manage your money so you can compete and profit in the sit-and-goes that you've learned about in this book.

BUY-IN BANKROLL

Twenty buy-ins is the conventional bankroll a poker player is expected to have in order to play regularly in sit-and-goes. For example, if you choose to play regularly in online sit-and-goes that cost $22, you should have a bankroll of $440 ($22 x 20 = $440). This means that you set aside $440 from your personal savings that you are willing to lose in order to earn a profit playing sit-and-goes. The twenty buy-in rule is effective because any poker player can run into a streak of bad luck. Bad luck combined with poor play can result in the loss of many buy-ins in a very short period of time. The twenty buy-in rule helps ensure that you don't go broke and dip into your personal savings, or wait for your next paycheck to play poker. When you are sufficiently bankrolled, you are usually able to play confidently because you are not concerned about going broke. And with a proper bankroll, you are able to stay focused on playing good tournament poker.

To play sit-and-goes as a business the way you have learned in this book, I recommend that you set aside twenty buy-ins before you begin to play your first Level A sit-and-go. This does not include the cost of traveling to a big buy-in event, or other expenses such as hotels and food. These twenty buy-ins are strictly for playing in Level A sit-and-goes. Therefore, in order to begin your journey toward a top-two finish in Level B for a big buy-in tournament with Level A sit-and-goes that cost $170, you should set aside $3,400 ($170 x 8 = $3,400).

As I mentioned earlier in the book, winning a Level A satellite after five buy-ins is a reasonable objective. One reason I think you should set aside enough money for twenty Level A sit-and-goes instead of five is that you might run into some bad luck. You may be an excellent sit-and-go player who averages a win in Level A after every three buy-ins in the long run. However, in case you experience a stretch where you keep losing key races or you suffer a number of bad beats, you may need a few extra buy-ins to get back on track and win your next level A.

Another reason twenty buy-ins is the right number is that you might find this tournament process very different from any other you've played before. As a result, for your first big buy-in tournament, there might be an adjustment period that will cost you more buy-ins than your long-term average for winning level A.

TRACKING RESULTS

Another key component of good money management is tracking your results. Doing so will help you evaluate your long-term profit potential by using the process you've learned in this book. Wouldn't you like to know if you are able to win Level A sit-and-goes on average every three, four or five tries? Or, on average, how much profit you generate on heads-up deals you make in level B? A good way to keep track of your results is to simply write things down in a notebook or keep them in an Excel spreadsheet on your computer. After each sit-and-go you play, make sure you mark down the result and record the date so you can track your results over long periods of time.

Now let's take a look at an important element in making a profit at any type of poker—calculating your pot odds.

12 CALCULATING YOUR POT ODDS

WHAT ARE POT ODDS?

The concept of pot odds is a very simple mathematical tool to help you decide if you should continue playing your hand. By enabling you to compare the cost of playing your hand to the amount of money you can win, it ensures that you don't overpay when you are considering putting your money in the pot. Let's say an opponent makes a $50 bet into a pot of $90 when you are holding J♦ 10♦ on a flop of K♦ 7♦ 4♣. The question that you need to answer is whether calling to complete your flush draw is the right play based on the price you are getting to look at the next card. However, before we can answer that question we first need to understand a few other important things.

CALCULATING THE ODDS OF IMPROVING YOUR HAND

To understand how pot odds work, you need to understand how to improve a poker hand by hitting one of your outs. Hitting an out means that one of the cards you need to improve your hand comes off on the turn or river. An example of this is seeing the J♥ drop on the turn when you are on a heart flush draw (for example, you have 9♥ 7♥ and the board is 2♥ 8♥ K♠ J♥). Another example is seeing the 2♠ drop on the river when you need it to complete a gutshot straight (for example, you have A♥ 3♣ and the board is K♣ 4♦ 5♦ Q♠ 2♠). In the first hand, your outs were nine hearts that were available in the deck to complete your flush. In the second hand, your outs were four deuces in the deck to make your straight.

In order to know the pot odds in any hand you play, you will need to count your outs and calculate the odds of hitting one of them on the turn or river. The Rule of 4 and 2 is a well-known shorthand method for calculating the odds of improving your hand. It works like this: When there are two cards to come, you multiply your number of outs by 4 to get the approximate chance of improving your hand. With one card to come, you multiply your number of outs by 2. For example, if you are holding 6♦ 5♦ on a flop of K♣ 8♠ 7♥, you have eight outs to make a straight (four fives and four nines). Assuming you get to see both the turn and river cards, you have about a 32 percent chance of improving or about 2.1 to 1. Assuming you get to see only the turn card, you have about a 16 percent chance of improving or about 5.3 to 1.

> ## THE RULE OF 4 AND 2:
>
> With two cards to come multiply your number of outs by 4 to get the approximate chance to improve (e.g. 8 outs x 4 = 32%). With one card to come multiply your number by 2 (e.g. 8 outs x 2 = 16%).

The following is a list of drawing hands you can use to familiarize yourself with counting outs and calculating the chances of improving a hand. Each example is listed with the corresponding number of outs to improve the hand, followed by the two hole cards, the flop, the approximate percent chance to improve the hand with two cards to come and with one card to come, followed by the cards needed to improve the hand.

BIG DRAWING HANDS

#	TYPE OF HAND	OUTS	HOLE	FLOP	CHANCE TO IMPROVE		CARDS NEEDED TO IMPROVE
					W/1 CARD	W/2 CARDS	
1	Flush draw and open-ended straight draw	15	7♠6♠	A♠8♥5♠	60%	30%	9 spades, 3 nines, 3 fours.
2	One pair and a flush draw	14	A♦4♦	9♦8♣4♥	56%	28%	9 diamonds, 2 fours, 3 aces.
3	Flush draw and open-ended straight draw	15	7♠6♠	A♠8♥5♠	60%	30%	9 spades, 3 nines, 3 fours.
4	One pair and a flush draw	14	A♦4♦	9♦8♣4♥	56%	28%	9 diamonds, 2 fours, 3 aces.
5	Flush draw and a gutshot draw	12	K♥7♥	9c8♥5♥	48%	24%	9 hearts, 3 sixes.
6	Top pair and open-ended straight draw	10	10♠9♠	10♣8♥7♥	40%	20%	4 jacks, 4 sixes, 2 tens.
7	Two overcards and a flush draw	9	Q♣J♣	9♦6♣3♣	36%	18%	9 clubs
8	Two overcards and open-ended straight draw	8+	Q♥J♠	10♣9♣2♥	32%	16%	4 kings, 4 eights
9	Double belly buster	8	8♥6♠	10♦7♠4♠	32%	16%	4 nines, 4 fives.
10	Open-ended straight draw	8	5♦4♦	Q♥3♠2♠	32%	16%	4 sixes, 4 aces.
11	One pair and a gutshot draw	6	9♠8♦	9♠7♠5♥	24%	12%	4 sixes, 2 nines
12	Two overcards	6	A♥Q♠	J♠8♦6♥	24%	12%	3 aces, 3 queens
13	Gutshot straight draw	4	10♣5♥	J♦9♠7♠	16%	8%	4 eights.

Hand 6. Top pair and open-ended straight draw. Even a loose player might be careful if he hits his 9 kicker, which gives him two pair but creates an open-ended straight draw on board, so he might not consider a 9 as an out.

Hand 7. Two overcards and a flush draw. You have at least nine outs, and possibly 3 queens or 3 jacks if your opponent is holding a lower pair, assuming his kicker isn't a queen or jack.

Hand 8. Two overcards and open-ended straight draw. You need 4 kings or 4 eights, and possibly 3 queens or 3 jacks if your opponent is holding a lower pair, assuming his kicker isn't a queen or jack.

Hand 11. One pair and a gutshot draw. You have at least 6 outs (4 sixes and 2 nines), plus possibly 4 eights.

DRAWING HANDS: OUTS AND ODDS

While The Rule of 4 and 2 is a terrific shorthand method to calculate the probability of hitting one of your outs, and while you will take advantage of its simplicity when you are playing, you should know that it isn't perfectly accurate. With two cards to come, you can get a more precise percentage by multiplying your number of outs by 4 and subtracting the number of outs in excess of 8. For example, with 13 outs and two cards to come, here is your chance to improve: 52 – (13-8) = 47 percent, or about 1.1 to 1. This discrepancy versus the Rule of 4 and 2 really exists only when you have nine outs or more with two cards to come. Once again, the best approach when you are playing is to just use the Rule of 4 and 2, knowing that the percentages are approximate but close enough to allow you to make the best decision.

Now let's go back to our original question about whether calling to complete your flush draw with J♦ 10♦ on a flop of K♦ 7♦ 4♣ is the right play based on the price you are getting to look at the next card. Here is how you answer that question.

There are nine diamonds left in the deck to complete your flush. Since you are considering whether to call to see only the turn card at this point, you need to calculate the odds with one card to come. With one card to come, you have about an 18 percent chance of hitting a diamond, or about 4.5 to 1.

The next step is to compare the pot you could win against the price you have to pay to win it. Your opponent bet $50 into a pot of $90 so there is now $140 in the pot, and it is costing you $50 to call. Therefore, you are getting 2.8 to 1 on your money ($140 ÷ $50 = 2.8). The final step is to compare the odds you are getting on your money, which are 2.8 to 1, to the odds of hitting one of your outs, which are about 4.5 to 1. Since you are getting nowhere near the 4.5 to 1 you need to make the call, you cannot call just to hit a diamond.

Let's review the steps for calculating pot odds:

1. Count your outs
2. Calculate the odds of hitting one of your outs
3. Divide the pot by the price you have to pay
4. Compare the result in step 3 to the result in step 2. If the result in step 3 is smaller, you are not getting the right price.

Notice that in our example, I concluded that you cannot call just to hit a diamond. What I meant is that while you are not getting the right pot odds to call, there could be other reasons for you to call. For example, if your opponent is all-in when he makes his $50 bet, there would be no more betting if you call. In that case you would get to see both the turn and river to complete your flush. Once again, you would have to look at the pot odds to see if calling is the right play. With nine outs and now two cards to come, you would have about a 36 percent chance of hitting a diamond, or about 1.8 to 1. Since you are getting 2.8 to 1 on your money, calling would be the right play.

Assuming your opponent isn't all-in, you could call if you plan on bluffing your opponent on the turn or river in case you don't hit your flush. If your opponent is a novice, A-B-C type of player, he might get scared if the board looks something like this after the river: K♦ 7♦ 4♣ 5♥ 6♥. That would put four cards to a straight on the board so by betting into him or raising him on the river, you could convince him that you have a straight with either a 3 or 8 in your hand. If he is holding just a pair of kings, he might fold. Of course, raising your opponent on the flop in order to make him fold is another way you might try to win the pot.

13 CALCULATING YOUR IMPLIED ODDS

When I talk about pot odds as a tool to compare the cost of playing your hand against the amount you could win, I'm not actually telling you the whole story. If you think that by calling and hitting your card, you would have a good chance of winning an opponent's entire chip stack, you would need to look at the implied odds. These are the odds that truly take into account the total amount you could win. They are calculated the same way as pot odds, but instead of just adding the total amount of money currently in the pot, you assume that there will be a lot more in the pot later on.

Here is an example. It is the first hand of a World Poker Tour Level A satellite. There are ten players, the blinds are $25/$50 and you all have $1,200 in chips. The player who is under the gun raises to $175, another player in middle position calls, and everyone else folds around to you on the button. You look down at pocket fours. The chances are pretty good that at least one of your opponents is holding either a high or middle pocket pair, or a big ace like A-K, A-Q or A-J. If you flop a set of fours on a board that looks pretty good to one of your opponents, you might double up early in this sit-and-go.

So, you need to look at the implied odds. It is about 7.5 to 1 to flop a set. There is $425 in the pot and it is costing you $175 to call, so you are only getting about 2.4 to 1 on your money. However, if an opponent is holding a hand with which he would commit all his chips after the flop, you would need to factor all his chips into the formula. You would be committing $175 into a potential pot of $1,450, which includes the raiser's entire $1,200, the caller's $175, and the $75 from the blinds. This gives you about 8.3 to 1 on your money, which is greater than 7.5 to 1; therefore, according to the implied odds you should call. Another important consideration is that even if you miss your set and are forced to fold after the flop, you would still have $1,025 left, which is enough to compete, so you wouldn't necessarily be gambling your entire tournament away by making this call.

Notice the relatively limited upside when calling a bet with a flush draw even when you are getting the right pots odds. The reason is that an opponent sometimes will slow down and avoid paying you off when he sees that third suited card hit the board. That is why you don't often calculate implied odds when trying to complete a straight draw or flush draw. One exception is playing a tricky hand like a double belly-buster straight draw (10♥ 9♣ on a flop of Q♦ 8♣ 6♣). It is when you have a well disguised hand like a belly straight or a set that your opponents might think they have you beat and pay you off with all their chips.

14 HAND VERSUS HAND: ODDS AND PROBABILITIES

In a sit-and-go you will usually find yourself in a position preflop where you are contemplating calling an opponent's bet when one of you, if not both of you, is short stacked. This can often lead to committing all of your chips preflop, because when you or your opponent can't make a normal sized bet after the flop without going all-in, you will likely just decide to go all-in preflop. In situations like these you will need to know the odds of your hand winning against a range of hands that your opponent could be holding.

Here is an example. Let's say that six players are left in a Level A satellite and blinds are $100/$200. You are in the big blind with $2,300 in chips. A short-stacked opponent moves in on the button for $1,000 after the first three players have folded around to him. The small blind folds and you look down at Q♦ 10♥.

SITUATION

Blinds/Antes: $100/$200
You Have: Q♦d 10♥h
Money in the Pot: $1,300
Bet for You to Call: $800
Number of Players: 2

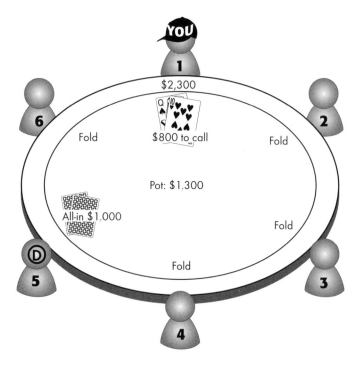

While Q-10 offsuit isn't a hand that you want to start playing big pots with on a regular basis, you have to consider that you could be getting the right price to call. So, you should calculate the pot odds and think about the hands your opponent could be holding.

You are getting about 1.6 to 1 on your money. Seat 5 on the button is in a pretty good spot to bluff since Seats 2, 3 and 4 all folded in front of him and he only has the blinds to worry about. He is also getting short-stacked so he needs to steal a few blinds in order to survive. In other words, there are a number of hands he could be holding that you are actually beating with Q-10 offsuit. If he has two undercards like 9-8 offsuit, you are actually about a 1.7 to 1 favorite and about 1.5 to 1 if his cards are suited. If he has a dominated hand like 10-9, you are ahead by about 3 to 1.

Now let's look at how your hand stacks up against a number of hands that you are not beating. If he pushed with a weak ace like A-9 or lower, you would only need 1.4 to 1, so you would be getting the right price to call. If he pushed with a 9-9 or lower, you would only need even money because you would be in a coin flip situation, so you would easily be getting the right price. If he pushed with A-J or K-J, you would need 1.7 to 1, so you would pretty much be getting the right price.

Of course, if he pushed with a dominating hand like A-Q, K-Q, Q-J, A-10 or K-10, you would need 3 to 1, which you are not even close to getting. If he has J-J, you would be behind by about 2.3 to 1 so you wouldn't be getting the right price. Also, if he happens to have a dominating pocket pair like aces, kings, queens or tens, you are obviously not getting the right price.

Now you should sum this all up so you can come to a decision. There are five hand groupings he could reasonably be holding that give you the right price to call—bluff with any two undercards, dominated hand, weak ace, small pair, A-J or K-J. By comparison, there are only three hand groupings that would have you in pretty big trouble, but it would be coincidental if the short stack in this spot turned over some of the really powerful hands like A-A, K-K, or A-Q. Also, even if you make this call and lose, you would still have $1,500 left, which is enough to compete. Finally, in Level A satellites, you need to find opportunities to gamble intelligently to accumulate chips because blinds that increase quickly and only first place wins the Level B voucher.

Therefore, given the price you are getting, calling is the best decision in this spot with Q-10 offsuit. As it turns out, your opponent has the A♣ 2♦, which means that you are behind by less than 1.4 to 1 and by making this play, you are getting good value for your money. The board comes 4♦ 4♥ 5♣ Q♠ 8♠ and you knock your opponent out.

Feel free to reread this example. It is important to understand the thinking that went into this decision because it will help develop your risk management skills. Remember that whether you are facing a bet or putting your opponents to a decision with a bet, you will often need to evaluate how much of a favorite or underdog your hand could be in case you have to get it all-in preflop. Knowing this will help you understand whether you are getting the right price to play your hand given how much is already in the pot, or how much you anticipate will be in the pot.

The following is a table of hand versus hand probabilities and odds that you can use as a guide. Work on memorizing it since you won't likely have a chance to refer to it when you are playing. In time and with more experience, you will come to instinctively know the outcomes of hand versus hand confrontations.

PROBABILITIES AND ODDS OF HAND VS HAND		
	PROBABILITY	**ODDS**
Severely Dominated Hand:		
A♦A♣	93%	13.3 to 1
A♠K♥	7%	
Dominating Pocket Pair vs Lower Pocket Pair:		
Q♦Q♣	82%	4.5 to 1
9♥9♠	18%	
Overpair vs Low Suited Connector:		
K♠K♣	77%	3.3 to 1
7♦6♦	23%	
Dominating Unpaired Hand:		
A♦K♣ (5% chance of tie vs any other unpaired Ace)	71%	3 to 1
A♥J♠	24%	
Pocket Pair vs One Overcard:		
10♣10♦	71%	2.4 to 1
A♠7♥	29%	
Overcards vs Undercards (Unsuited):		
K♥Q♦	67%	2 to 1
7♣2♠	33%	
A♣K♠	63%	1.7 to 1
10♦9♥	37%	
Winning Hand Unpaired (both cards beat opponent's kicker):		
A♠J♥	63%	1.7 to 1
K♦10♣	37%	
Winning Hand Unpaired (kicker is lower than opponent's two cards)		
A♠9♥	58%	1.4 to 1
K♦J♣	42%	
Pocket Pair vs Overcards (Unsuited):		
8♣8♦	53%	1.1 to 1
A♥K♠	47%	
Notes: • Suited cards increase in probability by +3% • 1% chance of tie is rounded out		

15 CLOSING COMMENTS

You don't have to win a major international tournament and become a household name to make a business out of playing poker. It can be difficult to consistently get strong results in multi-table tournaments against hundreds of players due to the countless factors that can affect your outcome. That is why the sit-and-go satellite strategies in this book are so valuable. Along with cash games and online sit-and-goes, they provide you with a reliable, fun and exciting opportunity to build your poker profits.

The purpose of playing poker is to make money. The purpose of reading books, participating in online forums, and subscribing to instructional poker websites is to learn new concepts so your game can evolve and you can continue to make money in the long run. Of course, the game should also challenge you and provide you with endless hours of enjoyment. Hopefully, reading this book has not only opened you up to strategic concepts that will improve your tournament game, but also introduced you to a new revenue stream that will grow your long term profits from playing poker.

Even if you don't regularly play in live satellites for big-money events, you will be able to apply the online sit-and-go methods you have learned in this book and start to see steady cash growth in your online account.

You now have a great new way to generate profit!

APPENDIX A

FLOP ODDS AND PROBABILITIES

FLOP ODDS & PROBABILITIES		
	PROBABILITY	ODDS
1 Pair, 2 Pair, Trips, or Quads with 2 Unpaired Cards::		
K♦ Q♠ on K♣ 8♦ 4♦ flop	33%	2 to 1
Set or Quads When Holding Pocket Pair:		
7♣ 7♦ on J♥ 7♠ 2♥ flop	12%	7.5 to 1
A Flush Draw When Holding 2 Suited Cards:		
A♣ 4♣ on Q♥ 10♣ 7♣ flop	11%	8.1 to 1
2 Pair Using Both Unpaired Hold Cards:		
J♦ 9♠ on J♣ 3♦ 9♦ flop	2%	48 to 1
Trips Using One Unpaired Hole Card:		
A♦ 6♣ on 10♠ 6♦ 6♠ flop	1%	73 to 1

APPENDIX B

OVERCARDS ON FLOP— PROBABILITIES AND ODDS

OVERCARDS ON FLOP - PROBABILITIES & ODDS		
HAND	PROBABILITY NO OVERCARD ON FLOP	ODDS OF NO OVERCARD ON FLOP
KK	77%	0.3 to 1
QQ	59%	0.7 to 1
JJ	43%	1.3 to 1
10-10	31%	2.3 to 1
99	21%	3.8 to 1
88	13%	6.5 to 1
77	8%	11.7 to 1
66	4%	23 to 1
55	2%	53 to 1
44	<1%	162 to 1
33	<1%	979 to 1

GREAT CARDOZA POKER BOOKS
ADD THESE TO YOUR LIBRARY - ORDER NOW!

DANIEL NEGREANU'S POWER HOLD'EM STRATEGY *by Daniel Negreanu.* This power-packed book on beating no-limit hold'em is one of the three most influential poker books ever written. Negreanu headlines a collection of young great players—Todd Brunson, David Williams. Erick Lindgren, Evelyn Ng and Paul Wasicka—who share their insider professional moves and winning secrets. You'll learn about short-handed and heads-up play, high-limit cash games, a powerful beginner's strategy to neutralize pro players, and how to mix up your play, bluff and win big pots. The centerpiece, however, is Negreanu's powerful and revolutionary small ball strategy. You'll learn how to play hold'em with cards you never would have played before—and with fantastic results. The preflop, flop, turn and river will never look the same again. A must-have! 520 pages, $34.95.

POKER WIZARDS *by Warwick Dunnett.* In the tradition of Super System, an exclusive collection of champions and superstars have been brought together to share their strategies, insights, and tactics for winning big money at poker, specifically no-limit hold'em tournaments. This is priceless advice from players who individually have each made millions of dollars in tournaments, and collectively, have won more than 20 WSOP bracelets, two WSOP main events, 100 major tournaments and $50 million in tournament winnings! Featuring Daniel Negreanu, Dan Harrington, Marcel Luske, Kathy Liebert, Mike Sexton, Mel Judah, Marc Salem, T.J Cloutier and Chris "Jesus" Ferguson. This must-read book is a goldmine for all serious players, aspiring pros, and future champions! 352 pgs, $19.95.

SUPER SYSTEM *by Doyle Brunson.* This classic book is considered by the pros to be the best book ever written on poker! Jam-packed with advanced strategies, theories, tactics and money-making techniques, no serious poker player can afford to be without this hard-hitting information. Includes fifty pages of the most precise poker statistics ever published. Features chapters written by poker's biggest superstars, such as Dave Sklansky, Mike Caro, Chip Reese, Joey Hawthorne, Bobby Baldwin, and Doyle. Essential strategies, advanced play, and no-nonsense winning advice on making money at 7-card stud (razz, high-low split, cards speak, and declare), draw poker, lowball, and hold'em (limit and no-limit).This is a must-read for any serious poker player. 628 pages, $29.95.

SUPER SYSTEM 2 *by Doyle Brunson.* SS2 expands upon the original with more games and professional secrets from the best in the world. New revision includes Phil Hellmuth Jr. along with superstar contributors Daniel Negreanu, winner of multiple WSOP gold bracelets and 2004 Poker Player of the Year; Lyle Berman, 3-time WSOP gold bracelet winner, founder of the World Poker Tour, and super-high stakes cash player; Bobby Baldwin, 1978 World Champion; Johnny Chan, 2-time World Champion and 10-time WSOP bracelet winner; Mike Caro, poker's greatest researcher, theorist, and instructor; Jennifer Harman, the world's top female player and one of ten best overall; Todd Brunson, winner of more than 20 tournaments; and Crandell Addington, no-limit hold'em legend. 704 pgs, $29.95.

CARO'S BOOK OF POKER TELLS *by Mike Caro.* One of the ten greatest books written on poker, this must-have book should be in every player's library. If you're serious about winning, you'll realize that most of the profit comes from being able to read your opponents. Caro reveals the secrets of interpreting *tells*—physical reactions that reveal information about a player's cards—such as shrugs, sighs, shaky hands, eye contact, and many more. Learn when opponents are bluffing, when they aren't and why—based solely on their mannerisms. Over 170 photos of players in action and play-by-play examples show the actual tells. These powerful ideas will give you the decisive edge. 320 pages, $24.95.

Order now at 1-800-577-WINS or go online to: www.cardozabooks.com

GREAT CARDOZA POKER BOOKS
ADD THESE TO YOUR LIBRARY - ORDER NOW!

PLAYING NO-LIMIT HOLD'EM AS A BUSINESS *by Rob Tucker.* In one of the most powerful poker books to come along in the last few years, this book shows you how to make consistent profits in both online and live cash games. You'll learn how to wait for big hands with which to trap opponents and avoid all the marginal and high-risk trouble situations that lead to losses, plus powerful strategies to outmaneuver and consistently beat aggressive Internet-style players and other tough opponents so you can *immediately* start winning money session after session. Tons of examples and graphics illustrate the winning concepts you'll need to beat no-limit hold'em cash games. 320 pages, $19.95.

THE POKER TOURNAMENT FORMULA *by Arnold Snyder.* Start making money now in fast no-limit hold'em tournaments with these radical and never-before-published concepts and secrets for beating tournaments. You'll learn why cards don't matter as much as the dynamics of a tournament—your position, the size of your chip stack, who your opponents are, and above all, the structure. Poker tournaments offer one of the richest opportunities to come along in decades. Every so often, a book comes along that changes the way players attack a game and provides them with a big advantage over opponents. Gambling legend Arnold Snyder has written such a book. 368 pages, $19.95.

POKER TOURNAMENT FORMULA 2: Advanced Strategies for Big Money Tournaments *by Arnold Snyder.* Probably the greatest tournament poker book ever written, and the most controversial in the last decade, Snyder's revolutionary work debunks commonly (and falsely) held beliefs. Snyder reveals the power of chip utility—the real secret behind winning tournaments—and covers utility ranks, tournament structures, small- and long-ball strategies, patience factors, the impact of structures, crushing the Harringbots and other player types, tournament phases, and much more. Includes big sections on Tools, Strategies, and Tournament Phases. A must buy! 496 pages, $24.95.

CHAMPIONSHIP NO-LIMIT & POT-LIMIT HOLD'EM *by T. J. Cloutier & Tom McEvoy.* New edition! The bible for winning pot-limit and no-limit hold'em gives you the answers to your most important questions: How do you get inside your opponents' heads and learn how to beat them at their own game? How can you tell how much to bet, raise, and reraise in no-limit hold'em? When can you bluff? How do you set up your opponents in pot-limit hold'em so that you can win a monster pot? What are the best strategies for winning no-limit and pot-limit tournaments, satellites, and supersatellites? Inspired advice you can bank on from two of the most recognizable figures in poker. 304 pages, $19.95.

CHAMPIONSHIP HOLD'EM *by T. J. Cloutier & Tom McEvoy.* New edition! Hard-hitting hold'em the way it's played *today* in limit cash games and tournaments. Get killer advice on how to win more money in rammin'-jammin', kill-pot, jackpot, shorthanded, and full table cash games. You'll learn the thinking process for preflop, flop, turn, and river play with specific suggestions for what to do when good or bad things happen. Includes play-by-play analyses, advice on how to maximize profits against rocks in tight games, weaklings in loose games, experts in solid games, plus tournament strategies for small buy-in, big buy-in, rebuy, satellite and big-field major tournaments. Wow! 392 pages, $19.95.

HOW TO BEAT SIT-AND-GO POKER TOURNAMENTS by Neil Timothy. There is a lot of dead money up for grabs in the lower limit sit-and-gos and Neil Timothy shows you how to go and get it. The author, a professional player, shows you how to reach the last six places of lower limit sit-and-go tournaments four out of five times and then how to get in the money 25-35 percent of the time using his powerful, proven strategies. This book can turn a losing sit-and-go player into a winner, and a winner into a bigger winner. Also effective for the early and middle stages of one-table satellites. 176 pages, $14.95.

Order now at 1-800-577-WINS or go online to: www.cardozabooks.com

POWERFUL WINNING POKER SIMULATIONS
A MUST FOR SERIOUS PLAYERS WITH A COMPUTER!
IBM compatible CD ROM Win 95, 98, 2000, NT, ME, XP

These incredible full color poker simulations are the best method to improve your game. Computer opponents play like real players. All games let you set the limits and rake and have fully programmable players, plus stat tracking, and Hand Analyzer for starting hands. Mike Caro, the world's foremost poker theoretician says, "Amazing... a steal for under $500... get it, it's great." Includes free phone support. "Smart Advisor" gives expert advice for every play!

1. TURBO TEXAS HOLD'EM FOR WINDOWS - $59.95. Choose which players, and how many (2-10) you want to play, create loose/tight games, and control check-raising, bluffing, position, sensitivity to pot odds, and more! Also, instant replay, pop-up odds, Professional Advisor keeps track of play statistics. Free bonus: Hold'em Hand Analyzer analyzes all 169 pocket hands in detail and their win rates under any conditions you set. Caro says this "hold'em software is the most powerful ever created." Great product!

2. TURBO SEVEN-CARD STUD FOR WINDOWS - $59.95. Create any conditions of play; choose number of players (2-8), bet amounts, fixed or spread limit, bring-in method, tight/loose conditions, position, reaction to board, number of dead cards, and stack deck to create special conditions. Features instant replay. Terrific stat reporting includes analysis of starting cards, 3-D bar charts, and graphs. Play interactively and run high speed simulation to test strategies. Hand Analyzer analyzes starting hands in detail. Wow!

3. TURBO OMAHA HIGH-LOW SPLIT FOR WINDOWS - $59.95. Specify any playing conditions; betting limits, number of raises, blind structures, button position, aggressiveness/ passiveness of opponents, number of players (2-10), types of hands dealt, blinds, position, board reaction, and specify flop, turn, and river cards! Choose opponents and use provided point count or create your own. Statistical reporting, instant replay, pop-up odds high speed simulation to test strategies, amazing Hand Analyzer, and much more!

4. TURBO OMAHA HIGH FOR WINDOWS - $59.95. Same features as above, but tailored for Omaha High only. Caro says program is "an electrifying research tool...it can clearly be worth thousands of dollars to any serious player. A must for Omaha High players.

5. TURBO 7 STUD 8 OR BETTER - $59.95. Brand new with all the features you expect from the Wilson Turbo products: the latest artificial intelligence, instant advice and exact odds, play versus 2-7 opponents, enhanced data charts that can be exported or printed, the ability to fold out of turn and immediately go to the next hand, ability to peek at opponents hand, optional warning mode that warns you if a play disagrees with the advisor, and automatic mode that runs up to 50 tests unattended. Tough computer players vary their styles for a great game.

---

6. TOURNAMENT TEXAS HOLD'EM - $39.95

Set-up for tournament practice and play, this realistic simulation pits you against celebrity look-alikes. Tons of options let you control tournament size with 10 to 300 entrants, select limits, ante, rake, blind structures, freezeouts, number of rebuys and competition level of opponents. Pop-up status report shows how you're doing vs. the competition. Save tournaments in progress to play again later. Additional feature allows quick folds on finished hands.

Order now at 1-800-577-WINS or go online to: www.cardozabooks.com

FREE!
Poker & Gaming Magazines

www.cardozabooks.com

3 GREAT REASONS TO VISIT NOW!

1. FREE GAMING MAGAZINES

Go online now and read all about the exciting world of poker, gambling, and online gaming. Our magazines are packed with tips, expert strategies, tournament schedules and results, gossip, news, contests, polls, exclusive discounts on hotels, travel, and more to our readers, prepublication book discounts, free-money bonuses for online sites, and words of wisdom from the world's top experts and authorities. Also, you can sign up for Avery Cardoza's free email newsletters.

2. MORE THAN 200 BOOKS TO MAKE YOU A WINNER

We are the world's largest publisher of gaming and gambling books and represent a who's who of the greatest players and writers on poker, gambling, chess, backgammon, and other games. With more than 10 million books sold, we know what our customers want. Trust us.

3. THIS ONE IS A SURPRISE

Visit us now to get the goods!

So what are you waiting for?

CARDOZA PUBLISHING ONLINE

GAMBLER'S BOOK CLUB

Shop online at the Gambler's Book Club in Las Vegas. Since 1964, the GBC has been the reigning authority on gambling publications and one of the most famous gaming institutions. We have the world's largest selection of gambling books—thousands in stock. Go online now!

702-382-7555
www.gamblersbookclub.com